CW00346621

YOU KNIT ME

YOU KNIT ME

A Memoir of Untangling Trauma to Create a God Woven Life

SANDI SAVAGE

You Knit Me

Published by: 4th St Publishing

Cover Photo: Tim Savage

Editor: Justin McCarty

For privacy reasons, some names, locations, and dates may have been changed. This book does not replace the advice of a medical professional. The information in this book was correct at the time of publication, but the Author does not assume any liability for loss or damage caused by errors or omissions. These are my memories, from my perspective, and I have tried to represent events as faithfully as possible.

ISBN: **979-8-9884055-0-4** (hardcover), ISBN: **979-8-9884055-1-1** (e-book), ISBN: **979-8-9884055-2-8** (paperback) Printed in the United States of America

To my sweet Josephine:

My love. There are things in this book that may be hard to read about mamma. Just know that my greatest ever accomplishment was you.

You are fully loved by me, your daddy, God, Jesus, and the Holy Spirit. Your mamma's life is a story of what can happen when things go really, really bad but then a really, really good Savior comes along. He took my tangled messy life and knit it into a beautiful tapestry of our family.

Thank you for being my daughter. You're loved more than you will ever, ever know.

Contents

Preface XI

Prologue XV

1. My Old Kentucky Home 3
2. High School, Hairspray & Beyond 15
3. Summer Drama at the Beach 25
4. Go-Go in Ohio 31
5. Gone to Carolina 39
6. The Audition 49
7. The Birth of Lauren St. James 53
8. Crack, Chaos, and Clubs 65
9. International Adult Entertainer 75
10. Vida de la Muerte 85
11. Martha Stewart of Mexico 91
12. A New Kentucky Home 105
13. When God Whispers Your Name 111
14. AD in HD 121
15. Becoming a Savage 133
16. Tell Your Husband 145

17. Un Cortadito Por Favor 163
18. The Beach and Bar Songs 173
19. The Birth of a Savage 185
20. Remembering the Promises 197
Afterword 209
Acknowledgements 211
Thoughts 213
About the Author 217

Preface

Perhaps I should begin by clarifying that my story probably doesn't look like yours. Everyone is unique, but I've had more than my fair share of unusual experiences — some through my own doing and some through the action of others. Regardless, I realize my story is not the norm and I'd like you read with that in mind.

So while you may not find a lot of "normal" in these pages, my prayer has been that you would discover hope. I share these experiences, not to sensationalize them, but so you can borrow courage from my history for yours. Whether it's in the moments where I felt alone, discouraged, abandoned, forgotten, abused, or betrayed, or in the places where hope, joy, peace, and resilience were knit into me, draw encouragement for your own life.

We often traipse through our days feeling alone, carrying the weight of experiences and feelings that isolate us. Mostly everyone you ever met has withered under the old lie, "No one else could possibly understand." My hope is that perhaps we can dismantle that ancient trap together. We each have a story — a wide array of painful things that have transpired in our lives leaving us hurt, angry, or betrayed — but if we will be honest and vulnerable about it, we will discover that none of us are alone.

Even more importantly, none of us have to be defined by it. When we pursue healing, we can emerge stronger human beings, growing in love, patience, and compassion for others. Believe me, though, that's not a quick fix. This book was a nine-year project, one that I kept coming back to, but had to put down periodically because I kept discovering things in me that needed healing before they could be written. At times, I wasn't even that enthused about finishing it, but the "still, small voice" in my heart kept telling me to push forward and see it through.

As a memoir, it's good to keep in mind that some of the names, places, and circumstances have been changed or tweaked in order to protect the identity of other people. After all, this is my story, not theirs. In fact, I want to be utterly clear — these are *my* memories of the events of my life. Someone else's memories of a certain incident may not look the same as mine. People tend to have different perspectives of what happened in a given situation, so this book represents my perceptions of events and how they shaped me in becoming the person I am today.

There are resources at sandisavage.com/gethelp in case you find yourself triggered or in similar circumstances that I encountered and need practical help in navigating through them.

Friend, reaching out to someone is the best thing that you can do when you are struggling.

Remember, we are *never* alone. Even when people let us down, there is a God who loves us deeply, eternally, and without fault.

> "*And I am convinced that nothing can ever separate us from God's love. Neither death nor life, neither angels nor demons, neither our fears for today nor our worries about tomorrow—not even the powers of hell can separate us from God's love. No power in the sky above or in the earth below—indeed, nothing in all creation will ever be able to separate us from the love of God that is revealed in Christ Jesus our Lord.*" (Romans 8:38-39 NLT)

Prologue

A Funny Thing Happened On The Way to the Porn Convention

I LOOKED AROUND THE hotel lobby in South Florida, and all I saw was a frenzy of people looking to buy an experience.

The industry was sex. Toys, costumes, videos, and magazines littered the area. Strippers, models, porn stars, porn consumers, men wanting sex, women wanting money — everyone wanting to be loved.

It was all I ever wanted.

The deep desire that had led me to this place had been the unrelenting ache to be loved by someone. Anyone. I wanted to be protected, treasured, and adored. I wanted someone to calm my fears, tell me everything was going to be okay and take care of me. But until that moment arrived, I needed to take care of myself, so I hatched a plan.

It was perfect. I just needed to start a pornography company with a friend of mine, buy a brothel on the outskirts of Mexico City, and I was set. Everybody's dream, right?

But it wasn't a pipe dream to me. I knew I could run that business better than anyone I knew. I had seen it all. I would spend hours a day watching porn when my boyfriend left the house, fueling my own addiction under the auspices of "research." I had zero doubt that I could craft better storylines, hire the best people, and churn out high-quality entertainment for people who "needed" it.

But one issue lingered in my mind. I couldn't escape the nagging thought that I was supposed to be doing something different. Something inside me whispered that I was made for something else, perhaps *anything* else. For a long time, I had not been able to put my finger on what it was, so I moved forward in the only way I knew.

Now my mind was racing. *How did I end up here?* A few days ago, I stepped off a plane after a six-week trip to England with my bestie. Now, I was standing in the middle of a gigantic room in a black bra, five-inch heels, and a blue silk scarf I'd picked up in Iceland wrapped around my hips. *What am I doing here?*

I suddenly needed to be out of that room. I was making my way through the hotel lobby when a strange thought ambushed my mind:

I could escape.

I could just leave everything.

My heart skipped a beat. My mind argued. *Probably impossible.*

I walked out through the front doors and into the smothering South Florida heat. *Should I even go back to my home in Mexico?* There had to be something beyond the meaningless "success" I had achieved for myself.

My absentminded walk took me alongside one of the most notorious porn actors of all time. He looked happy; why wasn't I? I turned my gaze down a ramp leading up to the hotel and saw a picketer. In his hand was a large, handwritten poster bearing the inscription: "John 3:16."

What in the world does that mean? A prickly teenage memory surfaced about that verse reference: "For God so loved the world..." But it didn't seem to fit. Why all the picketing and judgment to represent a God of love? It made me more confused than ever.

I turned to the crowd nearby and pointed him out. We quickly dove into snide remarks about his life like old pros. The words, "I bet he never gets laid," tumbled out of my mouth.

But as soon as I said it, I felt like I had crossed some strange, unseen line. I knew I shouldn't be making fun of him, and I suddenly felt an unfamiliar pang of guilt. The truth now seemed to be staring *me* down. If I was making fun of him, I was no better than he was. We both were just passing judgment.

It was painful. But it was real. Real was good.

A resolve was building in my heart, and the thought came again, this time with stronger force:

I could escape.

I turned around, walked back inside, and began to rip out the seams of the plan I had patched together.

A new pattern was taking shape.

It was time to get out of this life.

YOU KNIT ME

PART ONE

For you created my inmost being; You knit me together in my mother's womb.

I praise You because I am fearfully and wonderfully made; Your works are wonderful, I know that full well.

My frame was not hidden from You when I was made in the secret place; when I was woven together in the depths of the earth.

Psalm 139:13-15 (NIV)

Chapter 1
My Old Kentucky Home

I WAS BORN IN 1971 IN THE SMALL town of Mt. Sterling, Kentucky, boasting a population of 5,083, according to 1970 Census records. It has grown since but not by much. Mt. Sterling is "small-town Kentucky" and by all indicators, always will be that small, charming town. Kentucky was an "ancestral home" for me and I was blessed with a glorious, ever-growing family of aunts, uncles, and cousins, all undergirded by a remarkable generation of older women - my grandmothers.

These women were, without a doubt, my childhood "besties": my maternal grandmother, Memaw Dicy, my paternal grandmother, Memaw Lula, and later, my stepfather's mother, "G" (short for "Grandmother"). My mother and father divorced when I was four, so Mom and I went to live with Memaw Dicy for a short time. Memaw was a pureblooded Kentuckian, hailing from Prestonsburg in the hills of Eastern Kentucky where she had raised a family.

I loved my Memaw and she loved me. Even when mom remarried later that year, I would spend my days after school with her while she worked at the shoe store on

Indian Mound Drive. I would play in the backroom, savoring the crisp smell of all the new shoes on display. Memaw was a remarkable salesperson; she could fit the perfect shoe on anyone who walked in the door. She taught me to cook, crochet, sew, and fish - a truly amazing Kentucky woman. I remember playing with the prominent veins in her hands, poking and prodding them while watching her crochet massive blankets for us, and asking her again and again to see her "cards". She had saved all of the cards people had sent her over the years - some glittery, some flowery. I loved them all. I would sit by her rocking chair, looking at them, playing with them, and getting lost in the twinkling beauty of those cards.

On special days she would get out my mom's wedding dress from the back of her closet and let me try it on. I would stand in mounds of white lace and fabric, feeling like a princess. I couldn't wait to be a bride someday. Walking down the aisle in flowing silk clutching a bouquet of flowers seemed to be the very idea of perfection. Memaw also knew her plants. She had a variety of flowers and types of mint planted around her little front porch that gave off the aroma of a hot summer day: purple violets, pink, orange, and yellow zinnias, and large mint plants. I would pick them for a bouquet of flowers to go with my mother's wedding dress. Memaw and I would pick clovers from the yard and tie them together to make necklaces and crowns. Her love and our laughter were the seams that held my childhood world together.

My mom remarried a man named Ford, and we moved into a trailer on his family's large Kentucky farm. Ford owned the farm with his two sisters, and after his father's death, he occupied the trailer on the property while the main house was the residence of his sister and her family. The historic home was a sprawling, picturesque Southern mansion held aloft with columns and flanked by towering, graceful trees. A gigantic weeping willow grew near the house and became one of my favorite places to be on the farm. Inside, the wood floors were polished to a high shine, creating an air of grandeur that greeted every guest. Each of my cousins had their own giant, immaculately decorated bedroom. One even featured luxurious white carpet and a fireplace.

Whenever we would drive down the tree-lined lane leading up to the farm, crest the hill, and enter the circular driveway, I would look at that magnificent house and pretend I lived there – not in the trailer behind it. Of course, I would feel guilty for wanting more than my family provided, but I honestly didn't understand why we were living in the trailer when we were all "family." But life in the trailer wasn't all bad. True, there wasn't much privacy, but our little family had a lot of love. I didn't get to see my biological dad much, but I loved him and my stepdad, too. They both tried hard to let me know they loved me, but I was just a little girl, oblivious to the complexities of being a stepparent.

The best times were in the winter. *Snow.* Our collie, Brownie, was allowed to stay inside with us during the winter cold, adding to the ever-growing anticipation of

Christmas. Paper snowflakes, fake snow, and snowflake patterns on the window prepared the way for Santa's arrival. I still remember when I finally gathered my courage to ask Mom if Santa was real. She asked if I really wanted the answer and, in a sudden change of heart, I blurted out, "No!"

To this day, I still get gifts from Santa Claus.

My favorite holiday was and still is, Christmas. We would spend Christmas Eve at the big house and exchange presents with all the aunts, uncles, cousins, and G (Ford's mother), who adopted me into the family as one of her own grandchildren and helped me feel like I belonged there. One Christmas Eve I developed a cough, so, during our annual party, G provided a homemade Southern remedy: a shot of bourbon.

I didn't just like it. I loved it. I wasn't even ten years old, but I loved how it tasted sliding down my throat. Funnily enough, my cough did go away, but the desire for another drink didn't, and I began looking for my next opportunity. Later that year, we were at a Fourth of July party at the local Country Club, waiting for fireworks, when out came the champagne. It was my moment. I acted as grown-up as possible and asked a family member if I could have a sip of their champagne. Success! The bubbles made their way down my throat, but instead of a rush, I just remember getting tired and napping on a couch until the party ended.

Alcohol made me sleepy, and I missed out on a party, so I didn't touch any again until I was 12.

The changing of seasons on a Kentucky farm was idyllic – even from a trailer. Frigid winter days would give way to spring as Ford and I shared long walks down the lane looking for acorns, tasting spring onions that grew wild on the side of the road, or picking honeysuckle that grew on the fence behind the trailer. In summer, I would master the art of swinging on the tire swing or hide out under the gigantic weeping willow tree near the farmhouse, pretending to be in a fairy tale. I ran everywhere; through the fields as fast as I could or down the lane to my favorite hiking spot where I could search for baby mice to serve as pets. I belonged in the wild surroundings of the farm; it kept my heart and mind full.

One day a state official came to our house and walked me through some educational testing. We did the testing in the big house. Shortly afterward I was placed in a state program for gifted students at my elementary school. We were the original Geek Squad – the creative, high-IQ nerds. It seemed like someone finally understood how my brain worked: I needed increased stimuli and abstract learning, I needed to have independent projects to work on aside from the normal day-to-day school routine, and I needed mentors and teachers that could keep me engaged in active learning. It was the first time I looked forward to school and truly enjoyed my teachers. We did special projects, read advanced materials, and were a tight-knit crew. We even performed in school talent shows together, covering a few Blondie tunes and creating projects week after week. However, a few years later, the state discontinued the program due to funding issues, and, predictably, my grades dropped.

Then, one glorious day, we moved. We left the trailer behind and took up residence in a genuine *house* on the back of a gorgeous 1,000-acre Kentucky farm. Ford and Mom were eager to surprise me with the house, so I didn't see any of their fixer-upper work along the way. The first time I walked through the doors carrying my pint-size suitcase, I thought I had entered a palace! The floors were covered in a plush, dark brown carpet, and the rooms were spacious and roomy. The staircase right in front of the entrance looked so inviting. I counted each step. *One, two, three...* all the way up to 12. And there, at the top of the stairs, was the door to my *very own bedroom!* To my right was a dresser sandwiched between two twin beds, and to my left was another doorway into the adjoining playroom and storage area. The bed arrangement never stayed the same for long. Bunk'd (sleeping on top one night, down below the next) or separate (alternating beds each night) – the possibilities with those beds were endless. Perched atop this new house, I even had my own window, overlooking a tree in our side yard. I was ecstatic; it was like I had received a personal answer to my most heartfelt prayer.

Outside my room on the second floor was a heavenly-smelling cedar closet and a spare bedroom. Until my siblings were born, I had the run of the house, bouncing back and forth between the two bedrooms. Ford and Mom let me paint the rooms over and over again in the craziest colors to help express my creativity: peach, purple, and even eggplant (which is a totally different shade than purple, mind you). During my angsty teenage years, I once painted my room a dark charcoal color, one shade away from black, and then wrote poetry over every inch of the walls. Artsy, I know.

As much as I loved color, the thing that most captured my imagination and fed my soul was music. I would fire up my record player, don a pair of oversized headphones, and drift away to the sonic genius of Olivia Newton-John, Sheena Easton, and Laura Branigan. In elementary school I joined every singing-related program I could find and fell in love with the school choir. My teacher constantly urged me to sing softer so I funneled my passion into outdoor performances walking around the woods behind our house. I distinctly recall recording myself singing to the crickets – at least they didn't mind I was loud.

Since I was discouraged from being myself when singing, I transitioned my school music activities to band and dedicated myself to the flute. I loved the beautiful glow of the silver when I removed it from the blue velvet-lined case. Making music was such a place of profound mystery and wonder to me, and I would mesh my love of the outdoors and music by practicing the flute while walking through the fields on the farm. My love of science fiction was blossoming as well with my monthly subscription to *Omni* magazine, dreaming of the stars and how artificial intelligence could someday become a reality. I'd disappear into alternate universes through books like *Dune* by Frank Herbert and *The Lion, the Witch, and the Wardrobe* by C.S. Lewis. I even started writing my own little fiction book that I was sure would be a best-seller. Anywhere I could escape reality was where you would find me.

The farm was undoubtedly beautiful, but it was also remote. *Very* remote. The nearest neighbor was a considerable drive away, and reaching civilization had to be a planned event. I'm not kidding: we had our own gas pump on the property so we could fuel up before we left the farm. Living that far out, grocery runs weren't frequent, so we grew most of our own food. The main garden we dug out was the size of a football field, with a smaller garden planted behind the house. We spent the summer and fall months planting, weeding, harvesting, and canning produce. Memaw Dicy and Mom taught me to grow tomatoes, corn, peas, and beans, and I loved being with them, learning from them, and enjoying the long afternoons together.

But it wasn't all just gardening. Some days we would go fishing down by the creek. Memaw preferred the cane pole. I had a fishing pole with a button release and casted it like a pro. Memaw would bring two large mason jars with her, one sloshing with sweet tea and another brimming with cold chunks of watermelon, and we would sit on the creek-bank for hours, fishing and talking. Later in the evening, Mom and I would sit on the porch swing, wrapped up in a blanket while Memaw crocheted, all of us enchanted by the sounds of crickets and the dance of fireflies in the yard.

Ford was a tobacco and cattle farmer and worked hard, waking early every morning and working well into the dusk hours, so we didn't see much of him during the days. I begged to work with him when I could so that I could be with him. However, when he chose "washing and waxing the trucks and tractors" for our project, it wasn't as heartwarming as I'd hoped.

I also worked in the tobacco fields, pulling baby tobacco plants and replanting them in new areas. This was a role with serious upward mobility. As a rookie, I followed the tractor and ensured all the holes were filled with tobacco plants. I would jump into action if someone missed getting a plant into the setter.

Once mastered, I moved into manning the setter itself. There were four coveted seats facing backward behind the tractor, each occupant charged with the responsibility of pulling baby plants from a bin and slotting them into a rotating wheel that carried them down to the ground. Each plant would be watered at the time of implantation and stand up straight, ready to grow. A job on the farm that allowed you to sit down the whole time was a rare gift, but the sunburn that went along with it evened things out.

Topping the mature tobacco and harvesting was beyond my pay grade at the time, so other workers transported the stalks to massive tobacco barns on the farm, where they would be hung upside down on tobacco sticks from rafters to begin a curing process before moving into the stripping phase. This is where I re-entered the picture. When winter began, cured tobacco was moved to a small room near the barn, and we would stand at tables and strip, sort, and bale tobacco in the chilly air. That was life on the farm: planting, caring, pruning, growing, harvesting, repeat.

When we could make it off the farm, we went to church. At eight years old, I went to Vacation Bible School, and by the end of the week, I was praying along with everyone else to "become a new creation in Jesus." I begged Mom to let me get baptized. Weeks later, I got the green light and was baptized in the large baptismal pool behind the church pulpit. While greeting my family afterward, G gave me a small white Bible with my name embossed in gold on the cover. I attended church as often as I could, even joining the choir and participating in the youth group when I was older.

The whole era was a time of wonder, discovery, family, friendship, and faith. But, around age 10, I had my first introduction to pornography when I ran across a stack of magazines. I was confused by what I saw, but the women in the images looked glamorous and happy. The experience planted a seed in my mind about how a woman should be, a seed that would reap a truly damaging harvest later in my life.

Sexuality continued to darken my world as I got older. At age 12, an older boy in our church youth group took an interest in me, and in an effort to please him, I was easily induced to do whatever he said, including getting utterly drunk on vodka and orange juice at his house one day. One night, between choir practice and youth group, we snuck into a secluded part of the building and attempted to have sex. To be clear, it was merely an attempt; we didn't actually have sex. However, as a twelve-year-old, I still wasn't entirely sure how women got pregnant and became deeply frightened that I might have "caught pregnancy." The following day I went to a trusted teacher at school and told her about the experience and my fears of becoming pregnant. Later that same day, a school employee came to our music room and slipped the teacher a note, instructing him to send me outside. The teacher I had confided in was waiting at the door and immediately whisked me off to a nearby doctor's office for a pregnancy test. When I arrived back at school, the rumors were spreading like wildfire. *Have you heard about the twelve-year-old pregnant girl?* My world quickly unraveled. The school office contacted my mom, kids made merciless remarks behind my back, and the social shunning began. At home that evening, my very pregnant mother sat me down in my room and honestly asked, "Is it because you want to be like me?" Strangely enough, no one ever actually pressed for more details on what had transpired between the older boy and me. It took three years of living with a soiled reputation and then actually losing my virginity at 15 to realize that I had never even had sex.

It didn't matter; the damage was done. In order to teach everyone the lesson at my expense, I was removed from the church choir, kicked out of the youth group, and banned from future contact with the older boy. The first Sunday back to church I felt the eyes of everyone around me as I sat in the loft, stripped of my flowing blue choir robe, with my head hung low.

Punishment.

I knew then that this was to be the cost of every public mistake: exclusion, the loss of opportunities, the destruction of reputation. Nursing my fresh wounds there in the loft pew, I meekly accepted a tissue from G to wipe my eyes and decided never to attend church again.

Chapter 2

High School, Hairspray & Beyond

It was 1986. The year of yellow eyeshadow, yellow lip gloss, and big, BIG hair — and I was a freshman in high school. Although I was in high school, I was surrounded at home by younger children. By graduation, we had welcomed the rapid–fire arrival of five kids by my mom and step-dad and my dad and step-mom into my blended family (2 sisters and 3 brothers) — all of whom were born from the time I was 12-17. Since I was already bursting at the seams to build a life of my own, being a much older sister in a crew of youngsters made me feel a bit like the odd bird, so I threw myself into whatever I could that held out the promise of significance.

What does a creative mind do when chronically under-challenged? It strives to create a personalized version of the perfect life; it builds a fantasy life in which you are the star player. For me, it all centered around band. After my 12-year-old social shunning, I immersed myself in marching band and orchestra, claiming First Chair along the way. I stood unrivaled on the pinnacle of dorkdom. I found a group of creative, wonderful friends, and we spent enormous amounts of time together in classes, practices, band camp, and other events. I loved learning new music, hearing the sounds of our instruments as we warmed up, and then hitting that one glorious single note in unison to ensure we were in tune. The moment the band director's wand would start bobbing up and down, I would get lost in the sounds. And for a small town without much to celebrate, there was a surprising number of parades. As a "bandie," parades were torture for us. We cooked inside thick blue and white band uniforms under blistering heat and high humidity, counting steps and sweating our way through the streets. Cheerleaders danced and twirled in front of us while making snide remarks. It was the best of times and the worst of times.

After skipping English class to hang out with a boy during my sophomore year, I was demoted to last chair, the lowest ranking spot on the team, and familiar feelings of exclusion came rushing back in. I funneled my anger into competitiveness as the band director pitted me against other flautists to regain my seat. During the first week, I moved up a seat, and in the second week, I took down that amateur as well. For ten weeks, I continued my climb to the top until I regained First Chair: the prime spot, the best flautist, the go-to soloist. It was a sweet victory but shot through with offense and anger due to the humiliation of punishment.

Inspired by my own efforts, I began experimenting with other creative opportunities and took an elective class in Speech and Drama. In addition to the band, I took to the speech circuit as well and absolutely loved it. I found unexpected freedom and joy in diving into different characters to become someone else and welcomed the new escape outlet. Our team traveled around the state, competing in a variety of categories: debate, dramatic interpretation, duo, and poetry. Our teacher was hard on us but persistently prodded us toward excellence, resulting in award after award.

At one of those illustrious tournaments, I met my future best friend, my "bestie", Greg. I had taken up the habit of smoking cigarettes to calm my nerves before a competition and would search the different school grounds to find a suitable hiding place to take a drag before the competition began. At this particular school, I had zeroed in on the boiler room staircase for a quick puff when I heard footsteps approaching. I immediately threw my smoldering Salem Slim Light down, crushed it with the toe of my box-shaped black heels, and hid. I peeked around the corner and realized it was Greg, my competition nemesis. He consistently took first place with his highly dramatic performances. I squinted my eyes, took a deep breath, and yelled, "Hey!" just for the thrill of seeing him jump — which he did with a highly-satisfying squeal. With mock outrage, I gasped, "*Smoking*?".

He hastily dropped his fresh cigarette and turned to look at me. With a cackling laugh, I said,

"Me too. Let's have one together."

And thus began a 35-year friendship.

Along with smoking, I had also developed a regular habit of sneaking drinks from our family's liquor cabinet. The time alone on a 1,000-acre farm was a wonderful respite for a naturally introverted person like me, but it also created plenty of room for a wild fantasy life when coupled with readily-available substances to medicate a rising level of insecurity and anxiety. My drinking increased, and I sought friendships with people who were older than I was, some of whom had recently graduated. Additionally, after securing my spot as a teacher's pet, I was even allowed to relax in the teachers' lounge, where the teachers and I would sit and talk together, drinking coffee and smoking. Interestingly, this sense of camaraderie led to some undeserved grade adjustments and resulted in a positive bump in my GPA along the way.

When school ended for the day, I began spending time at a local business where a past crush, David, was involved. The friends I discovered there were older than me, and I was mesmerized by them. I even began developing a friendship with David that transformed into what I believed was "first love." While I had experienced a couple of boyfriends before, this was different. This was a guy I thought understood me. We would share conversations for hours, laughing and chain-smoking until I thought I would throw up. I was convinced — he was into me.

But there was one problem: his girlfriend. When he eventually made the decision to stay with her, my drinking skyrocketed, insecurity tightened around me, and I began hiding real feelings of despondency behind the mask of a smile that left everyone assuming I was completely fine.

In the late 80s, Mom and Ford finally built a house closer to town. When we moved in during my senior year, I felt a new sense of freedom, fueled by a steady stream of sugar and hairspray. I would squeal down the asphalt roads in my blue and white Chevy Blazer, sporting hair teased high, drinking Ale-8 (a locally-brewed ginger ale soft drink), and gulping down a box of Crunch n'Munch for breakfast. My 17-year-old metabolism enabled me to compulsively stress eat and still clock in at 97 lbs; I was blissfully adding one addiction after another.

Despite the fact that I maintained a high GPA, competed in national speech tournaments, and won a national band competition with a magnificent solo, high school graduation was a welcome sight. I had waffled on attending college, but after making a few friends at nearby Morehead State University, I finally submitted my application just a few weeks before the semester began. I was genuinely excited. Greg, my nemesis-turned-bestie, would be there and the Theatre and Speech program was incredible. I would still be close enough to Mt. Sterling to visit my family yet not right down the street. Of course, at this late stage in the game, they didn't have a dorm room available for me. Undeterred, I got resourceful and capitalized on the fact that a friend of mine was going to finally marry his longtime girlfriend so they could move into married housing, conveniently freeing up her spot in the dorm. He popped the question, they got married, and I got my room.

Although I wasn't sure what to expect at college, I grew convinced about what I wanted to do. The theatre crowd immediately resonated with me (these were clearly "my people"), and I loved the time I spent onstage, so I dove headfirst into every available play audition and theatre class I could find. I became such a permanent fixture around the department that the advisors started to take notice of me, fueling a quick rise through the ranks, which enabled me to secure parts in the most coveted roles. Although I truly enjoyed characters like Sissy in *Come Back to the Five and Dime, Jimmy Dean, Jimmy Dean,* the one I immersed myself in was the lead role in *Summer and Smoke* by Tennessee Williams. I played Alma, a repressed minister's daughter in love with the town doctor, and I still remember most of the lines to this day! It is one of the most significant female roles in theatre and kept me on stage 98% of the runtime, allowing only a few short breaks for costume changes.

Okay, can we just talk about costumes for a moment? I *adore* a well-made stage frock. Period dramas were my favorite costumes to don; the silk, lace, and adornments of a period costume make my heart happy. I would sit in the Morehead State costume shop, watching Cozy, our costume designer, sew pieces together with her tiny hands to make stunning gowns. It turns out the stage wasn't the only magical place in that building. When you walked down the hall from the black box theatre and into Cozy's shop, you were transported deep into realms of imagination. You could become anyone or anything you desired, and I deeply wanted to be someone else — not the girl who grew up on a farm, miles from anyone, pining after a man who didn't really want me, despite what his words told me. He was the Ashley to my Scarlett.

Life in the theatre department was one long afterparty. We wedged in classes around memorizing lines, staying out late, drinking way too much, and a smorgasbord of shenanigans. The theatre parties at Morehead were legendary; each one creatively themed, exquisitely prepped, and planned for weeks. Mornings were often marked by the "walk of shame" as I traipsed back up the hill to my dorm room, still costumed and slightly tipsy from the night before, rolling into bed for a few hours of sleep before class began. My friends were my go-to party partners and a frequent source of sustenance in tight times, especially Bestie Greg. When my small weekly allowance evaporated in cigarettes and booze, Greg would cover my lunch, springing for the two-taco blue plate special in the cafeteria. When that wasn't an option, chicken broth from a vending machine in the lobby of my dorm was another staple menu item. You would think no food seemed to be worth giving up my smoking habit. One day, after almost passing out from my slow-burn starvation, a theatre pal, Stacey, drove me home to Mt. Sterling so Mom could dish out some food, money, and a hot meal. That's what friends are for, right?

Between my freshman and sophomore years, I met my first husband, Trevor. We were far too young and much too different, but he had provided the attention I craved.

A week before our wedding, we stopped at a nearby swing set during a late-night walk and had a crucial, long-overdue conversation. Both of us questioned our decision to get married, but the invitations were already out — wasn't it too late? In our naivety, we trudged ahead rather than "cause a scene." Instead, the scene arrived on our honeymoon. After consummating our marriage, my new husband, thoroughly wracked with guilt, confessed to a drunken escapade at his bachelor party that resulted in sleeping with another woman the night before our wedding. My dreams of escape were crushed. I tried to make it work and forget his betrayal, but I couldn't. Living with Trevor in the married housing studio apartment was like being trapped in a cage. With resentment building every day, I stayed out late partying and working on shows, but the distance couldn't ease the pain. Later, we moved into a house with my friends, Stacey and Mona, under the auspices of saving money but primarily because I needed to be around anyone but him. By the end of my sophomore year, I couldn't handle the suffocating disappointment any longer, so we divorced.

With two years of college and a recent divorce under my belt, I wasn't sure what to do with the summer. I approached Cozy for advice, and after speaking with a friend at *The Lost Colony* Outdoor Theatre in Manteo, North Carolina, she secured a position for me as a seamstress. Off I went, no questions asked. I knew a few of the actors in the show, so I thought it would be a good place for me to spend the summer before the next semester. I waved goodbye to Morehead, my friends, my family and my past mistakes then headed to the sweltering coast of North Carolina. I was ready for a new fresh start yet I promptly stepped into a relationship and a decision that almost ended my life.

Chapter 3
Summer Drama at the Beach

My car, Scarlett, a cherry red 1981 Monte Carlo, went with my ex-husband in the divorce, so I carpooled down to North Carolina with cast members who attended Morehead with me. As a part of the cast and crew of *The Lost Colony*, housing was available at Morrison Grove. The apartments were nestled on a wooded hill with wooden staircases running up to individual cottages, Spanish moss hanging from swaying tree branches, and the salty smell of the ocean drifting in the air. When I pulled onto the property for the first time, I was a jumble of nervous excitement. Not only was this my first opportunity to live beachside, but relocating outside of Kentucky seemed like the fresh start that my soul longed for. With actors and creatives bustling everywhere, I felt like I had stepped into a romantic comedy, where just around the corner, my soulmate was waiting to absentmindedly bump into me as I lugged my suitcases from the car. As I found my tiny little room with an even tinier twin bed and unloaded my belongings, I was ready to make the most of my situation, including the job that brought me here — which I wasn't completely sure I could actually do.

Mornings started early. Costume repair from the past season was the top priority, along with costume fittings for all the new cast members. The glamour of show business was rudely interrupted by pricks from sewing needles that left my fingers raw and the near-constant drip of sweat in the thick coastal heat. We balanced out the hard work by hanging out at different cottages drinking and smoking late into the night to ease the monotony of it all. I had developed a hardy tolerance from my daily drinking habit at college, and as a 19-year-old divorcee among an older cast and crew, I fancied myself quite grown up and able to handle much more alcohol than I actually could.

Every day greeted me with a serious hangover from the exploits of the night before. No matter how much I drank, I couldn't get the thought of my ex-husband cheating on me the day before we got married out of my head. I deeply wanted to be loved, but that memory haunted me, making me feel unattractive and undesirable. So, in an attempt to regain my confidence and sense of self-worth, I resolved to snag as many men as possible that summer. All through my alcohol-soaked nights, I slept through the cast. I'd wistfully approach each new relationship wondering if this was the one that would finally make me feel happy and complete. With the sounds of James Taylor and the Indigo Girls flowing through my Sony Walkman, I'd wander from bungalow to bungalow looking for something that would satisfy.

However, there was one man who I couldn't seem to catch — Jimmie, the choreographer of the entire show. True, things about him were a bit of a mystery — he was older than me (does it really matter how much?), and he had recently separated from his wife under unclear circumstances (but who needs to pry?). The nagging glitch in my plan to bed him was that his "soon-to-be ex-wife's sister" was also in the crew. We were all in such close quarters that everyone knew everyone else's conquests from the night before. While I was sure he didn't want anything to get back to his wife, I had my target. So I hatched a plan. A "come as you're not" party was happening that weekend — meaning we all dressed up as someone we weren't, and people would have to guess our identity. I decided to make myself thoroughly unavoidable to this man and chose to dress up as *Jimmie*. So I donned my best leg warmers, headband, short shorts, and a tank top. I curled my hair like his and showed up on the doorstep of the party, knowing that it would cause a scene.

My plan worked. He came over and brought me a drink. We stood in a doorway talking while I downed a red Solo cup full of Mad Dog 20/20. Experience had taught me that if you copied someone's behavior while talking to them, they would feel more comfortable and gradually let their guard down. About an hour later, he was openly kissing me in front of the entire crew. Later that night, I moved into his cottage.

Our new relationship was fully out in the open, and I was immediately blacklisted by most of the cast and crew. The "19-year-old home-wrecker sleeping with the choreographer in full view of his sister-in-law" was not a popular role. I knew I had crossed some lines and felt the whispers of people talking about me behind my back, but I didn't care. I had succeeded in my plot to win this man's attention, and he rewarded me by showering me with all that affection I craved. He made me feel like I was wanted, needed, and valuable.

Weeks later, what was once mysterious started to become more apparent. Jimmie wasn't just "older"; he was 17 years older than me. A 36-year-old married choreographer taking an interest in a 19-year-old costume designer should have raised a red flag, but I didn't see it. I was far too "in love" to notice.

At the end of summer, the cast and crew hosted a talent show in order to showcase our abilities, and he choreographed a dance and dedicated it to me in front of everyone. It was the ultimate snub to those who had given us grief about our relationship. By the season's end, I was convinced he was absolutely in love with me and was ready to divorce his wife. As we parted, he assured me that he would be filing the paperwork and contacting me very soon. I thought that it would be best to stay nearby in North Carolina so that I could get to him quickly after he informed his wife of his intention to divorce. As the cast and crew departed from our summer accommodations, I stayed behind until Morrison Grove emptied out, and I found myself alone. When I finally did get in touch with him, he informed me that he was planning to give it one more try with his wife but that he had a "beautiful summer" with me.

Alone, with all my belongings in a black garbage trash bag, and approximately 48 hours from being homeless, I was stuck and desperate. So I called my old friend, David, in Kentucky and asked if he would come to pick me up. We had kept in contact and I clung to the hope that he would one day realize I was the one for him. The request was no small feat — a 13-hour drive down from Kentucky to North Carolina and 13 hours back again — but he said he would. The following night, as he pulled into Morrison Grove, I was overcome with gratitude that he came to rescue me. We talked for hours and ended up on the beach talking about the future late into the night. He asked me if I loved Jimmie, and though I knew I didn't — he had simply been a conquest — I wanted to hurt David's feelings and told him I did. I wanted him to think I had moved on, that I had gotten over him and the pain he had caused me - but I hadn't. I wanted him to fight for me, but instead, he slowly nodded his head, said, "Ok, then," and we headed back to the Bluegrass State. Despite the rescue, I once again felt trapped with no options.

Chapter 4
Go-Go in Ohio

ONCE WE ARRIVED BACK in Kentucky, I moved in with David, his wife, and another friend of ours. While wrestling with anxiety about my future, I started drinking more daily. I found comfort in vodka and in the subsequent drunken hazes, I began concocting ambitious plans for us all to succeed. The standout strategy for world domination was for David to practice law, but reality quickly crashed in when we ran out of money. We moved to a different city and we all crammed together into a tiny studio apartment. One room, four adults, zero cash.

Without any other viable options on the table, we collectively made the decision that the three women of the house would begin go-go dancing in a local club to earn enough cash to sustain the four of us.

The world of adult entertainment quickly opened up its arms to me.

I applied for a license to strip in Newport, KY but we decided it would be best if we moved a little further North to begin our new jobs. The club was located on the outskirts of Cincinnati in a town called Sharonville. The job was simple: get men to buy us alcohol. We would take turns dancing on a small stage behind the bar, complete with a pole, then come out, sit with customers, and ask for alcohol. The other women were 21, but, despite the fact that I was only 19, I was still expected to make a liquor quota. The girls and I would swirl around the pole, laugh, act like fun party girls, and then take home the cash. Our costumes consisted of eye-catching bras with matching thongs, but for the sake of decency, all go-go dancers wore pantyhose under their thongs. We would take little safety pins and pin the tops of the hose to the underside of our thongs, and I suppose it made me feel more covered up, not as exposed to strangers. Still, we were making a living. I never really gave the industry much of a second thought, telling myself,

I can always get out whenever I want.

The men that frequented the bar were much older, coming in to escape stressful days, nagging wives, and tough jobs; I genuinely felt sorry for them. And since my last boyfriend was 17 years older than me, the age difference didn't seem like a big deal to me. I developed friendships with "the regulars" and would sit and talk to them when I didn't feel like putting on the hustle. One customer, a man in his late 50s, was a sweet guy and shared with me how he felt alone in the world. He was a big guy, rode motorcycles, and stopped for a beer almost daily. When things slowed down in the bar, he became the guy I would consistently gravitate toward.

Meanwhile, our cramped studio apartment was becoming more and more dysfunctional, which tends to happen when you cram four adults into a small studio apartment together.

Working at the bar one evening, I felt particularly alone and outcast, so I turned to a bottle of Bacardi 151 to sort through my emotions. I still remember feeling the metal filter across the bottle top as I would take swig after swig straight from it. I drank so much that I threw up in the changing room but kept going. My tolerance was very high, but the same could not be said for everyone. With none of us able to drive, we ended up calling David to come to pick us all up. The events of that night became a tipping point of sorts for me. On the way home, I sat in the back seat and realized I didn't want to live with them anymore. It was unhealthy for us all, especially for my own heart, so I made a decision to leave.

Unfortunately, I was contemplating homelessness just a few weeks before Thanksgiving — not a heartwarming situation. Suddenly I remembered my "friend" from the bar — the old biker that had become my buddy. Surely he would understand! He would probably be glad for the company and offer me a place to stay while I figured things out. Fishing his number out of my things, I called him up. I was right. He quickly gave me directions to his house and said he'd call a cab and pay for it once they dropped me off. When I arrived at his place, it was an apartment above his sister's house and looked clean enough. I dragged my hastily-packed suitcase up the steps and took stock of my new surroundings. It was basically a kitchen and a bedroom.

The first few days were spent adjusting to life in a compact apartment, and the old biker was genuinely respectful of my space. I was pretty upset, unsure of my next step, and he seemed to understand that I was not interested in any kind of relationship with him. He kindly drove me to and from work, and I kept dancing. However, after the initial days passed, his temperament changed. He spelled out quite clearly the true price of "rent" — if I was going to stay any longer at his place, I was going to need to be his girlfriend — in every sense of the term. That night he sexually assaulted me. Suddenly I had a new decision to make — not just about my life — but *for* my life.

Over the next few weeks, I played the part, acting as if I was his girlfriend but secretly working out my plan. I would cleverly lead this man to believe that I was falling for him so that he didn't kick me out of the apartment, meanwhile stashing away as much money as possible to make an escape. "Survival sex" was the only path I could see forward — a pattern that would carry me through much of the future ahead.

Thanksgiving finally arrived. In my family, it was always a fancier event — polished silver, fine china, and some of your best clothes. In preparation for this new "family time," I put on a pair of slacks and a sweater, but when he walked in the door with a bottle of wine, he looked at me in disbelief.

"No, you can't wear that. You are mine, which means you've got to wear a biker t-shirt," he chided me.

I was mortified. I think it was some form of rebellion against his family to make us look like some rough biker crew. In disbelief, I slowly changed into a short sleeve t-shirt, a pair of jeans, and some black boots. We made our way downstairs and into his sister's house, which was lovely. The table was inviting and decked out for

Thanksgiving dinner, but I felt horribly out of place. I held back tears through the whole meal. As we finished dinner and retreated upstairs, I told him I couldn't do this anymore and that I was leaving. He angrily stalked outside and screamed at the top of his lungs in pain, as if he had desperately fallen in love with me and couldn't part with me. When he returned to the kitchen with tears running down his face, I told him I'd stay but internally solidified my exit plan. The ruse didn't work as well this time, though. He started locking me in the house unless I was at work and not letting me use the phone for fear I would leave.

Undeterred, I kept working the plan. And then, one day, I finally saw my chance. He had begun to loosen his grip, trusting me enough to leave me in the apartment while he went to the grocery. I knew I only had a short window before he returned, so I immediately dove for a long-distance phone card that one of my co-workers had slipped me. I had one person I thought I could call: Jimmie. True, he had gotten back together with his wife and was trying to sort through things with her, but I didn't know where else to turn.

I quickly dialed the phone, and thankfully, Jimmie answered. I explained my surreal circumstances that I was being held captive and needed to escape the apartment and leave town. I asked if I could stay with him in North Carolina until I figured out my next move, and without delay, he said, "Yes." At the moment, neither of us gave much thought to how his wife would receive that information, but I was desperate — I had to get out. He told me that a Greyhound bus ticket would be waiting at the local station in my name — I would just need to get there. He promised to be waiting in North Carolina at the station to pick me up. It was all the courage I needed to make my move.

By this time, I had accumulated a few hundred dollars, enough to pay for a cab to the bus station and plenty left over. I just had to make it through the night. When I woke up that morning, a fresh layer of snow had fallen, leaving the roads a bit treacherous but I didn't care. I knew if I didn't go, something could happen to me, and I would never be found. So after he left, locking the door behind him, I quickly began packing my suitcase, pausing only to ensure that I could no longer hear the sound of his motorcycle in the distance. Taking a deep breath, I broke out a window, crawled out, and ran through the snow, dragging my suitcase behind me. I didn't stop until I was several streets away, and then finally paused to catch my breath and my bearings. Tears flowed from relief.

I was out. I couldn't believe it.

I shakily called a cab from a nearby payphone, and they picked me up at the street corner then I was on my way.

Jimmie came through. A bus ticket was waiting there for me. My hopes were up — surely he would be at the other end of the trip to pick me up. Night slowly approached, and the time finally arrived to board the bus. As we pulled out of the station, I had the passing thought that I was free. I was rolling down the highway to freedom. Little did I know I was rolling into deeper dysfunction.

Chapter 5
Gone to Carolina

THE GREYHOUND PULLED INTO the station in Chapel Hill, North Carolina, and I nervously scanned outside the window to see if Jimmie was there. I began to panic, fearing that I was now stuck in a different state with nowhere else to go. And then suddenly, there he was. He smiled and looked relieved to see me. With a grateful cry, I ran and collapsed into a tight hug with him. My body sighed with relief, I knew I would be able to stay with him for as long as I wanted. The issues he was working through with his wife were no secret, but I was confident that I could make this arrangement work.

Confident? Maybe.

Clueless? Absolutely.

We arrived back at his apartment and walked up the stairs to find his wife standing at the door. She stated that she knew precisely who I was and that I could sleep on the floor of their spare bedroom. The room was entirely devoid of furniture, so she threw a few blankets into the room and told me to make myself comfortable — it was at least carpeted. That night I cried myself to sleep from the combination of sheer exhaustion, how she had treated me, and my longing for a better life after the nightmare of Cincinnati. In the middle of the night, Jimmie slipped into the room to sleep with me, huddled on the floor. It would be the only source of comfort over the next few weeks.

The details are a bit of a blur, but it didn't take long for the fighting to begin between the two of them. Anger, name-calling, and so many tears, but in the end, she left. Jimmie and I discovered this new development after a late night out, drinking together, when we waltzed into an empty apartment. She had taken everything they owned, all the way down to the toilet paper. Only one stinging memento remained — a painting of a gazebo in Manteo, North Carolina, where they were married.

I watched Jimmie crumble. He sat down on the floor and cried inconsolably. I tried to comfort him, but it felt wrong. I didn't want to comfort him about his wife leaving. It meant that we could finally be together and that was a good thing, wasn't it? I was 19 and utterly oblivious to what other people were experiencing. I had already divorced my first husband and now succeeded in breaking up Jimmie's marriage. However, it wasn't all that I had hoped for. We did move into the main bedroom, but with all the furniture gone, I still was sleeping on the floor. I was unsure of what was going to happen, but I believed it had to be good.

I was wrong.

For several weeks I played the wife, doing my part to help our new "family" by cooking and hunting down second-hand furniture to restock the apartment. Jimmie was a talented cook and he taught me some fantastic Italian dishes. I cooked endlessly while I sang out loud to take my mind off our empty bank account and the growing fear that we wouldn't make it. Meanwhile, Jimmie started teaching ballet classes. While it provided some money, I was disturbed by what I saw when I went by to visit. He looked *too* closely at the girls in there; he touched them in ways that didn't seem necessary. I confronted him and he said I was crazy — he was a ballet instructor and he had to touch them to show them how to hold their back and arms.

I was stuck. With nowhere else to go, I decided to believe him.

Not long after that, as I was rummaging for towels in our cramped little bathroom, I uncovered a stash of porn magazines and was utterly shocked. How was it that I was in a relationship with a porn addict? Staring at the images he had stashed between some towels, I suddenly felt like he had cheated on me and I instinctively threw up. As I sat there trying to recover, a deep, gnawing feeling took up residence in my gut, accompanied by an anxious question: *Why am I not enough?* Honestly, why did he have all of this pornography? I was young, beautiful, and smart; why would he need any of *that*? But obviously, he did, so I made the conscious choice to start changing my look and my behavior to match what he wanted.

However, I became increasingly unhappy with who I was, which led to a struggling relationship that was constantly on the brink of failure. One night, in the middle of a rainstorm, I walked across the apartment building parking lot to a nearby convenience store. The only thing on my shopping list was Mad Dog 20/20.

I walked back home and there in our apartment, sopping wet, I threw a handful of pills in my mouth, washed them down with a drink, and kept the full bottle nearby. I ran a bath and then laid down in the water, fully clothed, ready to end my life.

With the water splashing at the end of the tub, tears were streaming down my face.

What are they going to do if I succeed in dying?

I thought about my mother crying over my grave, never seeing my brothers and sisters again, not knowing my future nieces and nephews and what our family would grow to be like. I would miss all of it. The shock and pain of it brought me to my senses and I began to rethink my plan.

Ultimately, Jimmie came home and found me before I was able to harm myself. He promised that he would do better, that *we* would do better, and that he would try to make everything right. Over the following weeks, he did try to pay more attention to me. But when I realized it was just an attempt to make up for hurting my feelings, not because he genuinely wanted to pay attention to me, it left me feeling unimportant and unwanted. I knew he didn't love me and was using me, but I didn't see a way out. I felt oddly chained to him.

As the holidays drew near, a sense of excitement and hope began to build in me. That time of year had always been special to me, and now, I finally had a reason to go home and reconnect with my family. There was a whisper of a promise in all of it — somehow, everything was going to be okay in the world again. At Christmas, we made the journey back to Kentucky and stayed at my mom's house for the holidays. However, my alcoholism was now at full throttle and my drinking never seemed to stop.

During a late-night bender, I got a phone call from my old boyfriend, David. He asked if I would come and see him in a town about two hours away. Without question, I jumped at the opportunity to escape from Jimmie and his dysfunction for a day. The following afternoon, when I looked out the window and saw a limo driving up our gravel driveway, I was giddy with excitement. The driver whisked me off and I spent the two-hour drive to the hotel enjoying the space and growing in anticipation.

He spared no expense on the hotel; I was utterly impressed. I made my way up to the room and waited for him. When he arrived, we spent the evening eating, talking, and reminiscing. We found ourselves sitting on the floor facing each other, his back against the bed, my back against the floor-to-ceiling windows with snow starting to fall behind me. He told me how beautiful I was and it felt amazing — like someone actually saw and valued me. I phoned Jimmie and told him I wouldn't be back that night because of the snowstorm. The following day, on the limo ride back to my mom's house, I grew increasingly upset that I was allowing myself to be in a relationship with someone who made me completely unhappy. And yet, I felt trapped. My lack of money kept me from being able to see a way out and a smothering wave of depression washed over me before I arrived.

On New Year's Eve, I decided to attend a party with my bestie, Greg. Jimmie had started drinking early that afternoon, and I didn't want to be around him when the clock struck midnight, so I left him at the house with my parents. Around 11:00pm, while I was tearing it up on the dance floor, Jimmie called me and told me he was going to end his life. Completely drunk and utterly frustrated with how he was treating me, I told him, “Go ahead,” and hung up the phone. When I got home, he hadn’t taken his life but had passed out from drinking too much. The next morning, on the first day of a brand new year, he made his usual apology and promised to do better.

Following the trip to Kentucky, we decided that a change would be good for us, so we made the call to move. We sold the few belongings that we had, tossed Jimmie’s old camping tent in the car, drove to Nags Head, North Carolina, and pitched our tent in the state park — in the middle of a rainstorm. Thankfully, the rain didn’t get in the tent, but by the morning our site was swamped. We broke down the site and moved to higher ground, and later that day I went job hunting.

I interviewed at a furniture store full of all the beautiful things that I wanted in a home for myself and was astounded when I was actually offered the job. Each morning I would take a frigid shower at the campground and spend all day longing for the furniture I was selling to everyone else. I would have traded anything for an honest-to-goodness bed instead of laying my head on the ground in a tent and waking up every morning with back and neck pain. It did have trade-offs, though — opening the tent zipper in the morning and greeting the sunrise always gave me hope that something better in the day could happen. After a few weeks, Jimmie told me that a friend would rent us a room in their house, and I was elated! *Finally!* A real bed to sleep in.

My steady work started to bring in a small paycheck and Jimmie began teaching dance classes. We were both drinking heavily and passing out every night. Suddenly I started feeling sick and wasn't sure what was happening to me. I was waking up nauseated every day but thought it was due to a near-constant state of hangover. After a couple of weeks, it dawned on me that I could be pregnant and it scared me. Jimmie had always said he did not want children, and if I was pregnant, I had no idea where I would go or what I would do. I bought a pregnancy test, took a deep breath, and tested myself in the bathroom of the furniture store at work.

Positive.

I immediately found a phone book and looked up a place that said they would help women who were pregnant. After work, I drove to the little office on the outskirts of town, walked up a flight of steps, and entered a relatively bare room furnished with just a few chairs and a TV. When I let the woman at the desk know that I was pregnant and I needed help, she proceeded to show me a video of what happened when someone got an abortion. I had walked into a pro-life office that relied heavily on fear tactics to convince women to continue with their pregnancies. I got up in the middle of the video, screaming and crying, and ran out the door.

Later that evening, when I summoned the courage to inform Jimmie that I was pregnant, he got violent with me and told me that I had to get an abortion. I told him I didn't want to, but he said he didn't care. He drove me to my workplace and had me quit my job. From then on, he kept me locked in the house and never let me out of his sight. He forced me to call a relative to ask for money to be wired to me for the abortion, and once it was received, he threw me into the truck and drove across the state border to an abortion clinic. Before we walked in, he threatened to harm me if I didn't go through with it. A short while later, I was lying on a table in agony, crying and pleading with the doctors, "No, no, no, this is not what I want." But they went on with the procedure. Jimmie had told them he was my legal guardian and he was the one that would make the decision. After the little unborn life was ripped from me, he hauled me up into the truck and drove me back to our room, where I slept, mixing gin and nighttime cold medicine to numb my pain, crying for what seemed like days.

Without my income, Jimmie was not making enough money to support us, so we worked to come up with a plan to pay our bills and still eat. I begged him to move back to central North Carolina and we found a small one-bedroom apartment in Greensboro. But the day still finally came — we just didn't have enough money to pay the bills.

I made a decision then that I was going to be the one to take care of it.

I wanted to feel like I had control of my finances so that he could never make me do anything ever again. Around the same time, a Tears For Fears music video, "Woman In Chains," seemed to be speaking to me — it revolved around a woman taking care of her tortured man, and I began to wonder if perhaps I could take care of us by bringing in some money. I thought to myself: *I'll do it.* I knew I could go to a club and dance; I could be the one to take care of us. The world of adult entertainment had welcomed me with open arms before — I knew they would again. I reached out to a club and asked if I could audition, and they said, "Of course, come by this afternoon."

I had go-go danced in Ohio. How different could it be in North Carolina?

Very different, as it turned out.

CHAPTER 6
THE AUDITION

I CAN DO THIS. I can do this. I can do this.

I looked down at the heels that I knew were too short. They were black satin heels I picked up at Rack Room. I had on a black velvet dress I had gotten in college and it felt too long.

Okay. Pick a song.

"Diamonds and Pearls" by Prince.

"Do you want something to drink?"

"I'm underage. Just 19."

"It's okay. Don't worry, it will take away your nerves."

"Okay. Gin and tonic with bitters."

"For someone underage, you sure seem to know your drinks."

"You better believe it!"

Five gulps. Gone.

"Alright! Show me what you've got!"

1, 2, 3.

There are three steps that lead up to the mirrored stage with two poles in the back.

1, 2, 3.

I look at my feet to make sure I don't stumble up the steps. I shake my arms a little, flopping them at my side to shake off the rest of my nerves.

1.

I can do this.

2.

I have to make money. Jimmie isn't making enough as a dance instructor.

3.

It's just taking off a few more clothes than I did when I was a go-go dancer in Ohio.

The stage.

I look out at the manager. The first sweet sounds of Prince's voice are loud and beautiful over the speakers at the club. The managers, bouncers, bartenders, and doorman all watch as I slowly strip down to nothing.

I swing around the pole. I dance down the lit runway of the stage. I give it my all. I have to get this job.

The song comes to an end, and the owner walks up to the stage.

"Can you get higher heels this afternoon?"

"Yes."

"Can you start tonight?"

"Yes."

"You're great. You have a job." I finally felt in control.

PART TWO

CHAPTER 7
THE BIRTH OF LAUREN ST. JAMES

THE MANAGER LOOKED AT me and said, "Okay. So, you have to have a name that isn't yours. What do you want it to be?"

Everyone has a stage name in strip clubs. Primarily, it protects your identity with clients but also gives you a sense of freedom to become whoever you want to be. My background in theatre made it second nature to assume another identity and adopt a new personality. This was simply going to be a new role I was playing — the beautiful, smart stripper. And, of course, to find the right name, I dipped into the best place I knew: soap operas.

One of my family's all-time favorites was the daytime TV staple, *The Young and The Restless*. I still remember the first scene that I ever saw from the show — it was the 1982 season, and I was eleven years old. "Nikki" was working at a strip club when she met a wealthy man who fell deeply in love with her, whom she eventually married. Without ever realizing it, a seed had been planted in my heart early on. During the entire time I worked in the industry, I carried a deep longing and wish for some wealthy man to swoop in, fall in love with me, and rescue me from my financial woes. With that hope simmering in the background, I chose the name of a character from *The Young and The Restless* that was strong, didn't take crap from anyone, and displayed a fiery, tenacious personality: Lauren. My last name became "Saint James" — an ironic nod to my clear lack of saintliness coupled with an homage to the trauma I had endured from Jimmie, whose given name was James. And thus, "Lauren St. James" was born. A new name and a new identity to the world.

Within a few days, I was one of the favorites at the club. I was young, pretty, and desperate for money. I quickly learned all the tactics to get men to buy me alcohol (even though I was still just 19) and pay lavishly for dances. The music played hour after hour, enveloping and transporting me as it had always done, but this time it enabled me to lose myself and disassociate from the reality of what I was doing. When you work in a club, your performance is driven by a playlist of songs you choose, during which you progressively remove more of your clothing. When you come off stage, you then walk around and ask the men in the crowd if they would like a table dance. The rules of the city and state determine how close you can get to a customer and how many clothes you can take off at the table, so making real money was just a matter of getting men to buy drinks and making them feel important. I mastered all of it early on.

"Oh my gosh. Hi! I love that tie. You have such incredible taste. Do you mind if I sit down with you for a little bit and rest and have a drink with you?"

"Oh my gosh. You're so funny. I wish I could just have you around me all the time. Being around you makes me so happy."

"Oh my gosh. This is one of my favorite songs. Do you think I could take my clothes off for you?"

Manipulation became like a second language to me, and honestly, it didn't even take that much. The typical men who walked through the doors of the club felt unappreciated, unwanted, and unloved. As an adult entertainer, I learned to meet some of those needs in order to maximize profit. In a club, dancers are expected to give the house a percentage of their table money, and, beyond that, there's the obligatory tipping.

You tip the DJ so that they play the music you want.

You tip the managers so that they tell you who the good customers are.

You tip the bouncers so that they keep an eye on you and protect you when a customer gets unruly.

You tip the makeup artists so that your makeup looks great.

You tip the hairstylists so that your hair is always on point.

In Greensboro, at the first club that I worked in, I was treated well by the staff and had friendships with the other ladies in the club, but one of the bartenders was aggressive with me. More than once, he would call me into an office to grab me, prod me, poke me, or make me sit on his lap under the impression that if I didn't do what he asked me to do, he would get them to fire me. With my financial security on the line, I didn't complain about it. Instead, I pushed my feelings down and dealt with the consistent daily sexual abuse by drowning it in a steady diet of alcohol. When I started at the club, I was a gin girl but switched to vodka when I discovered it gave me less of a hangover and that I could mix it with different fruit juices to avoid the boredom of drinking the same thing every night.

Just like back in Sharonville, we had our regulars — men eager to build relationships with the dancers. If I was in the dressing room and a regular walked in, a bouncer would come back and let me know, "Hey, Frank just walked in. Make sure you put on a pretty dress." I would then go out, talk to him, ask how his day was, see if he needed to talk about anything, and then let him look at me naked, all the while telling him how wonderful he was.

Because the regulars could occasionally develop an intensely strong attachment to you as a dancer, the job requires some skill in psychology. After I'd been at the club for about six months, I noticed that a car parked at the gas station down the street belonged to one of my regulars, and he started following me on the drive home. I took the roundabout way and called the cops, but there wasn't much that they could do as he hadn't done anything. He continued to try and find out where I lived, but I would always throw him off track. Finally, one day after he threatened me at the club, the cops were able to come and take him into temporary custody, which scared him enough to keep him away from me.

While I was daily losing bit by bit of myself Jimmie stayed in his own world, teaching dance, drinking a fifth a day, and using my income to pay bills. I kept hustling and he kept coming up with more bills that we needed to pay. I rarely saw any of the money after I made it, but I trusted that he was paying off our debts.

One day, the owner of the club started building a room next to the main stage. When we asked him what it was, he said, "That's going to be the VIP Room, where our best customers can go. We're going to put all velvet couches in there and make it a beautiful environment for you ladies to do your job." I was genuinely excited.

Oh my gosh, this is going to make me more money, I would think to myself. But when that VIP Room opened up, the customers that we took in there, even the regulars, expected much more now that they were in a protected environment within the club. Outside the view of other customers, they thought they could take liberties with us. And many times, for more money, I allowed it.

The success of the VIP Room gave the owner courage to try something no one had ever tried before. For the first time in North Carolina history, we opened a topless carwash. It was located conveniently behind our strip club, and guess who got to open it up? You guessed it: me.

Now I'm sure you've got questions: so how does a topless carwash work? Well, it primarily operated like a normal drive-thru car wash but with some key differences. There was a bar inside, a few tables and customers were invited to sit and have a beer during the car wash (or stay in the car if they preferred), and while it was a first for North Carolina, it wasn't necessarily very different than what I was doing in the club. Just add cars, water hoses, and sunshine to the recipe and if you wanted to have a lap dance while you were waiting, well, of course, we would oblige. It was hard work though as we actually cleaned the cars. In heels. We vacuumed the carpets, hand washed the outside, made sure to detail the inside and added shine onto the wheels. On hot summer days, we would pop lawn chairs out behind the 10 foot barrier wall and work on our tan while waiting for our next customers. Sure enough when it was 5:10 p.m., there would suddenly be a line of cars 20 deep with men thinking their cars were dirty.

My nights started to blur together; the lights, the shows, the men. I would often arrive back to the apartment late into the night, having drunk way too much. I was driving around in our F-150, half-lit almost all the time, and I put a lot of dents and scratches in it. I was even consistently getting pulled over at night by the cops but would talk my way out of a ticket each time through flirting, a flash, a promise to take care of them at the club — anything.

At home, things were getting worse. Jimmie was addicted to porn, and one night after kicking off a late afternoon with a few cocktails, I tried to call Jimmie and couldn't get him to answer the phone. He was supposed to be at his parents' place, but there was no answer on the phone and I began to worry.

Did something happen to him?

And then, after a few more hours, I got mad.

Is he having an affair?

Did he find someone even younger than me, even prettier than me?

Why can't I get ahold of anyone?

I could not stop thinking about it, and the only place I knew to go for answers was his parents' house in Lenoir, North Carolina. Unfortunately, he had dropped me off at work that day, so he had our only vehicle. So what was a young enterprising girl going to do to find a ride? I called the regular cab company that was going to take me home that night and discovered that the drive from Greensboro to Lenoir would cost $300. Back then, that was an enormous amount for a cab fare, and I didn't have that kind of cash available. So I went to the VIP Room, charged triple to let one of our regulars cross lines with me, and walked out of the room five minutes later. I called a cab, and once it arrived gave them the address and passed out in the backseat.

Two hours later, the car arrived at Jimmie's parents' house late at night. I stepped out of the car, still drunk, onto fresh snow that had started to fall during my ride there. To my surprise, the house was locked, and no one was there. I suddenly realized that I didn't have access to any money to pay the cab driver for the two-hour return trip, so I asked him to leave me there at the house, confident that I could figure something out. In light of the freezing temperatures and the locked, vacant house, he protested. But I insisted and he eventually drove off. I looked at the house, walked around to the back door, took off my shirt and wrapped it around my hand, and punched a hole through the back glass door to reach in and unlock the door to let myself in. I proceeded to make my way to the back bedroom, where I usually slept when we were visiting his folks, and passed out.

The next morning, I awoke to Jimmie and his parents standing over me, furious.

"How in the world did you punch out the glass and break into the house — in the middle of a snowstorm — and think that this was okay?!"

I let him know I was worried because I hadn't heard back from him. It turns out that they had gone up to their condo in the mountains, where there was no phone service.

Wow, that would have been helpful information.

Despite their anger, his parents made me breakfast and then told Jimmie to remove me from their house and take me back to Greensboro. When we arrived home, I let him know that I thought it was time for us to move again. I had broken the rules at the club and was going to need a fresh place to work.

Later that month, we packed up our things and made the move to Chapel Hill, North Carolina. While we were packing, fresh hope surfaced in me. Maybe I wouldn't have to dance anymore; I could just find a regular job and be a "good girl." So after arriving in Chapel Hill, I applied to work at a bagel shop near the university campus and was hired. Fortunately, they didn't ask much about my past work history, assuming that a 20-year-old in a college town probably didn't have much work experience anyway.

I truly enjoyed working at the shop. I loved cooking and making people happy by providing good food. The camaraderie of our team was a joy and a welcome change. The people were genuinely nice to me and I was doing something that I felt like I didn't have to be ashamed of.

Just a few steps down from the bagel shop was a local bar that became a frequent hangout. The nearby location and regular karaoke nights made it irresistible. I would meet Jimmie after work and we would pound beers until we could barely see straight. After a night of heavy drinking, we were walking down the middle of the road in Chapel Hill when I chose to lie down because I was "too tired." In reality, I just wanted to escape my life. It was only because Jimmie pulled me out of the way in time that I wasn't run over by a passing car.

One evening, toward the end of my shift, as I was preparing to head over to the bar next door, the managers asked if I could come back over after closing time and talk to them about a couple of things. After several beers at the bar, I drunkenly made my way back over to the bagel shop for my conversation with management. They said they had overheard me telling one of my coworkers that I previously had a job I wasn't very proud of and then proceeded to ask me for details. With the secret out, I let them know I had been an adult entertainer.

The managers then informed me that I had only one opportunity to save my job: strip for them and give them lap dances. Without much recourse, I did. But after getting back home that night, I decided they couldn't fire me if I just never came back. After all, if I was going to be treated as a stripper at a normal job, I might as well be stripping in an actual club and making far more money, right? But before choosing to head back to the clubs, I clung to the hope that maybe there was still a way for me to make a normal living.

I could ask the darkness to hide me
and the light around me to
become night—
but even in darkness I cannot
hide from You.

Psalm 139:11-12 (NLT)

Chapter 8

Crack, Chaos, and Clubs

IT WAS TIME TO try a new job, so I decided to apply at a local gym. I was very nervous about going in, so I had a couple of beers before I went to the interview.

Let's just all agree that's a bad idea, okay?

The interview was off to a great start when the manager asked me if I knew how to operate the equipment. *Absolutely!* As an adult entertainer maintaining my physical appearance was essential, so I often went to the gym and was familiar with all the equipment.

"Okay, great. Show me"

I took hold of the first piece of equipment and ripped off a few quick reps like a pro. I stood up — and promptly passed out. The next thing I remember is waking up with smelling salts underneath my nose and concerned staff hovering over me.

They decided to pass on an offer.

Having struck out on two normal jobs, I made the decision to return to the adult entertainment industry and began commuting to different clubs back in Greensboro. My drinking rose to unprecedented levels. I was downing an entire bottle of something every night and then hopping in the car in the wee hours to drive back home.

During the day, Jimmie kept teaching classes, but on nights when I wasn't at the club, we would head to a bar and end up wasted as well. We finally decided that he would return to work as a chef with a friend of his, Giovanni. I would stop by Giovanni's restaurant on my days off and enjoy a bottle of red wine with his girlfriend while I waited for Jimmie to get off work. It was a welcome change.

Giovanni was a riot; he hailed from Sicily and would walk around singing to the customers in his restaurant. So when he decided to open an upscale restaurant attached to a strip club, I jumped at the opportunity to work with him. He employed me as one of the featured entertainers and I would spend my nights working the jacuzzi room, shower room, and main stage, surrounded by incredible food. On a really good night, a customer would ask us to dine in the restaurant. House rules stated that we would dress appropriately and have two hours to have a meal with our customers — a welcome break from the loud music and skin everywhere.

Alcohol had been my addiction of choice up to this point. I knew girls at the club that did drugs, but it wasn't really my thing. Jimmie, on the other hand, was a cocaine addict and he kept hounding me to join in with him. At some point, I finally gave in and told him, "Fine, call your dealer tonight." I did my first line of coke and felt invincible. The pain I was living with faded away; nothing could hurt me or get in my way — I was limitless.

Then morning came — and so did the crash.

I woke up alone and began scrambling to find the dealer's number.

"Is this normal? Am I dying? I feel like my heart is going to give out. I'm sweating, and I want to throw up."

He said, "No, that's just coming down off of the drugs. I'll come over and sit with you so you're not alone."

It seemed incredibly kind of him to bring over soft drinks and food and just sit with me. In hindsight, I realize it made me trust him, which actually led me to use more. I started calling him on a regular basis for cocaine. It helped me feel distant from the job that I was doing like it wasn't really me that was dancing, but someone else. However, one of the girls at the club ended up telling Giovanni I was doing coke, and I got suspended for a week. I hastily told Jimmie that we needed to make another move so that I could find work at a new club.

This time we landed in Myrtle Beach, South Carolina. I had been nursing a crazy notion that if we got married, perhaps things could be different. Surely he would change, he would become responsible, and we could start acting like grown-ups. After discussing it, we decided to make the drive to my hometown and tie the knot. Jimmie wore a suit, and I wore a brown skirt and blazer combo. We were married at the courthouse and, to celebrate, made rounds to every family member's house for drinks. By late afternoon, we were completely trashed. He decided to go back to my mother's house, and I stayed with my bestie, Greg, at my grandmother's house, where the three of us drank my grandmother's recipe of hot buttered rum well into the night. My first night being married to Jimmie, I didn't actually even see him.

It wasn't a great start to the big change in our lives, and from there, things started to get even worse. We resented each other. We were constantly drinking. Although my drug use was occasional at best due to the steady supply of alcohol provided by customers at the club, Jimmie's drug use started to escalate.

When we arrived in Myrtle Beach, I started working in a small club operated by a previous manager of mine from Greensboro. Because I knew someone, I was able to walk in the door and start without an audition. Jimmie and I found a trailer for rent, conveniently located near two bars. My tolerance was high, I was functioning at my job, and then one day, Jimmie brought home these little cream-colored rocks and told me to smoke one with him because it was even better than cocaine.

Convinced I could handle it, I took my first hit of crack cocaine with a "Why not?"

One hit wasn't enough, though; I wanted much more. When we smoked all we had, I became convinced that some had fallen somewhere on the floor. I ended up crawling around on my hands and knees, looking for any rock that could have fallen. At one point, I ran across a scrap of Kentucky Fried Chicken that we had eaten earlier that weekend and became convinced it was a rock. It took me some time to realize that a piece of crispy skin wasn't going to burn correctly, nor was it giving me the kind of high I was looking for.

Jimmie started doing drug runs to find more product for us, and at one point, he had me ride along with him. As we pulled up near another car parked on the side of the road, he pushed me into the floorboard and yelled, "Stay down!" While he spoke with the dealer, I stayed huddled on the floor, shaking in fear. When he got back in the car, he instructed me to stay down until we were out of sight. He said the dealer had told him to come alone and could have shot him if I had been seen. I was incredulous.

"Why in the world did you bring me with you then?"

"So you could see all I do for you and for us. I put myself in dangerous situations all the time — you should be thankful."

Crack was merciless. In three weeks' time, I almost died twice.

The first time was at a drug dealer's house. We had been doing crack all night long, and when I passed out, they repeatedly dunked me in a jacuzzi to revive me so they could avoid an uncomfortable visit to the hospital.

The second time I tried to run into the ocean to drown while I was high.

It dawned on me that I was not going to be able to continue doing crack and survive, so I decided to dial back to occasional cocaine use. However, I compensated by ramping up my alcohol use. After coming into work hungover numerous times, I lost my job at the small club and decided to move to one of the biggest clubs in the area.

I was hired immediately, but working at this club required a whole new wardrobe. It was an upscale establishment, so I needed multiple sequin gowns and plenty of rhinestone and pearl-studded undergarments. Management was strict on appearance and behavior. There were even weekly weigh-ins; if you weighed 10 lbs over, you were automatically suspended for a week until you got yourself back in the gym. We also were subjected to regular dressing room nail checks, during which everyone was lined up for fingernail inspection. If they didn't look perfect, you were asked to put on elbow-length gloves til you could have them fixed. My anxiety coupled with alcoholism would drive me to break the ends off my artificial nails while covered with the gloves and I'd play absentmindedly with the little pieces of acrylic. I'd dig them into the flesh of my fingertips when I was particularly anxious or needed to create a little pain to sober up. I'd stuff full length sequin gowns and all my accessories into a locker that was provided for us in the dressing room and flip open my caboodle stacked with makeup and glitter and hit the floor each night first stopping at the bar for liquid motivation. I quickly realized that I could finally make much more money there, and I saw the first opportunity to leave Jimmie and support myself.

I was given the opportunity to open several clubs for the chain across the country and, eventually, internationally. Our club network was well-known and frequented by movie stars, basketball players, comedians, and golf pros. My adult entertainment career skyrocketed. During a club opening in Memphis, Tennessee, we discovered that the stage had been poured incorrectly, and what should have been a two-week trip became a six-week extended stay. Jimmie was furious. He couldn't believe I would leave him alone for that long, forcing him to pay his bills on his own. When I arrived back at Myrtle Beach, he got in my face and threatened me through clenched teeth,

"I wish I had never met you. I wish that you were dead."

What had always been a risk became a growing fear of what he might do next.

We moved out of the trailer into another house with a roommate, just north of Myrtle Beach in the woods. Jimmie grew increasingly aggressive and angry, and his drug use spiraled out of control. In a private conversation with our roommate, I confessed, "I've got to try to get away from this, but I'm not sure how to do it." They urged me to believe that the right opportunity would come and to take the chance if I was that unhappy.

Over the next few months, I kept watching for that opportunity, as I steadily poured more energy into my career as a featured entertainer opening clubs across the country.

The moment finally arrived when management asked me to travel to the opening of a new club in Mexico City. At this point, Jimmie had become undeniably dangerous; he had stolen a gun from our landlord and was threatening to kill me, my entire family, and himself. I pacified him and told him I would only be gone for a few weeks. The club needed me to go open this place, but it would make us all the money we needed. It calmed him down enough to let me slip out of the country.

As I boarded the plane to Mexico City, I was convinced that this would be my opportunity to make the money I needed and figure out how I could legally divorce him. I had finally gotten away from him and I knew this was my chance to leave him for good. I could disappear in a city that size and I would even be protected at the club by bouncers — there was no way he could get to me.

The plane arrived at night and the city lights seemed to stretch on for hundreds of miles. My addictions were raging, I was on the run from an abusive husband, and I was crying tears of joy as the plane descended toward a gigantic city in a country I'd only seen in pictures.

**If I ride the wings of the morning,
if I dwell by the farthest oceans,
even there Your hand will guide me,
and Your strength will support me.**

Psalm 139:9 (NLT)

Chapter 9

International Adult Entertainer

BEFORE THE PLANE TOUCHED down, the knot began in my stomach.

What in the world am I doing in a different country?

I don't know the language.

I don't know the people I'm going to work with.

Ironically, it was the memory of the abuse I had escaped that calmed my current anxiety. Whatever was next couldn't be worse than what I was leaving behind.

As I walked off the plane and into the airport, I was overwhelmed by the number of people, cultures, and languages I encountered. Everything popped with color; it was vibrant, electric... *alive*. A driver sent by the club met me and transported me to a hotel next to the beautiful Angel of Independence statue on Paseo de la Reforma in downtown Mexico City. The drive there was more like a race; at least, I couldn't detect any traffic laws as we zipped in and out of our lane. The city at night was as beautiful and intriguing as the first glimpse I had gotten from the air. My excitement for the next month grew steadily during the drive to the hotel. I checked into my room and fell asleep quickly, sleeping soundly for the first time in a long while.

The next morning, another driver arrived and whisked me off to the club so that I could learn the rules and meet the managers, bouncers, staff, and some of the other entertainers. When I walked through the doors of the club, I was greeted by my female manager, who let me know that my passport was to be kept for safekeeping so that I didn't run the risk of losing it in a foreign country. At that time, it seemed like the wise thing to do; if I lost my passport, I was afraid I would never be able to get back to the United States. So I cheerfully handed it over, and she locked it in her office safe.

"Now, here are the standard fees that you pay out each night; the percentage of each dance that you give to the house. And once your quota is filled for the month, we will give you back your passport so you can return to the United States."

And then it hit me. In order to get my passport back, I had to make a certain amount of money. However, making money hadn't been a problem for me in the U.S., so I shrugged it off and went on a tour of the club.

The main front door was used by both the customers and staff, and flanking it was a pair of bouncers that would let staff and entertainers in and out each night. Due to the shared door, one standing rule was that entertainers were required to look their best even when walking into work. If customers were standing in line, or potential customers on the street saw us walk in the door, they would know we were quality specimens.

In the dressing room, we had access to a make-up artist and a woman who would make custom outfits for us to wear onstage like long velvet dresses, sequin gowns, elbow-length gloves, and the like. The costumes were just a part of our roles as entertainers, and I thoroughly enjoyed dressing to the hilt. To be completely transparent I still have a deep love for animal print, sequins, hair extensions and glitter. Since it was an international club there were women working there from all over the world: Hungary, the Czech Republic, England, the United States, and Mexico. I quickly became friends with a few of the girls and the staff. We were like a little family watching each other's backs.

I knew the routine. I tipped the DJs and had the songs played that I wanted; I tipped the bouncers, and they took care of me. I was a genuine joy to work with, no doubt.

There was only one problem: I was a raging alcoholic.

Once I started to dial into the regulars who frequented the club, I relaxed into the familiar role of entertainer and confidant, and my, how the drinks flowed! I would drink like a fish all night long, taking a break only to dance, and then stagger back to my hotel room and pass out.

When my month-long tour wrapped up, my manager handed me my passport and a plane ticket, telling me that I was always welcome back at the club. She knew my story with Jimmie and assured me that the door was open. I could simply call and she would have a plane ticket waiting for me at the airport.

With a plan forming in my mind, I asked if I could make a quick return to the States to keep my visa valid, and then immediately fly back, which she gladly arranged. I called and let Jimmie know that the club needed me in Mexico for one more month. I promised I would come back — that I loved him and didn't want to be there. I made him believe that everything was okay and not to worry. My escape plan was working! I was absolutely fine with leaving all of my possessions with him and starting over. I was finally free.

I threw myself back into life at the club, making a name for myself in Mexico and continuing my descent deeper into alcoholism and cocaine addiction. After another month went by, I let my manager know that I would like to stay in Mexico for an extended period of time. She agreed and made long-term arrangements with my hotel.

Now, with my new life anchored in Mexico City, I called Jimmie for the last time and told him that I was not coming back.

He was livid and unstable on the phone, one moment yelling, the next crying. I told him I thought it was best — that it wasn't him, it was me. I did my best to soothe and settle him down as much as I could, but I realized that it was not up to me to keep him pacified. Instead, my responsibility was to remove myself from an abusive relationship.

In the weeks that followed, I found out from my mom that he had written to her, trying to find out where I was. She responded that, unfortunately, she just didn't know the exact address. In the end, it took two years, but I was able to complete the divorce process through the mail, and at long last, he finally signed the papers — on Valentine's Day.

It was the best Valentine's Day gift ever.

Continuing to work in Mexico was a mistake, but at the time it seemed like a great plan. I was a "return girl" to the club, and the owners treated me differently than other girls. They housed me in a hotel nearby where I'd been the month before, but this time I had my own room that I no longer had to share with anyone. Every day I was picked up for work by a driver and dropped off at the club.

True, the nights were filled with grabbing, pinching, and rude comments from customers, but the staff appeared to care for me — after all, they threw out the rowdy customers and made sure I was doing okay. It felt like I mattered and was included in something, so I unknowingly began to overlook the legitimate physical abuse I was enduring every day. My arms and legs were full of bruises from men gripping me too hard. I started to believe a twisted lie that I was so desirable they couldn't help from marking my body with their want for me. I started wearing the bruises as badges. It was a step up from having to live with Jimmie, so it just seemed worth it. But it was not.

Each night I would step onstage and dissociate. My sense of self had become intertwined with the character I had worked to create, so I paid attention to every detail: shimmering glitter on my shoulders and face, awash in Victoria's Secret body spray, and knee-high platform boots that served as the sweaty cashbox for the wads of bills thrust upon me throughout the night. Once my costume was ready, I'd walk up the stairs behind the stage and mentally psych myself up to make the next 15 minutes unforgettable.

The familiar waft of beer, alcohol, and sweat would welcome me to the platform. Then, the quick burst from the fog machine while the DJ thundered, "Now, welcome to the main stage — Lauren St. James!" The familiar drum beat and guitar of one of my favorite songs, "Cherry Pie," would saturate the atmosphere — my cue to step out onstage and into the lights, feeling like nothing was in my way.

I longed for the applause, acceptance, and the feeling of simply being wanted that came with those moments. It almost didn't matter why it was being given. I would lose myself in the performance, blocking out the looming reality that I would soon have to talk to and dance for the men who waited for me. On a good night, one of the bouncers would sweep up all the bills that had been thrown at the stage as tokens of appreciation from my admirers in the room.

Backstage, I'd wipe the sweat from my brow and brace myself for what came next. *It's only for a little while,* I'd remind myself. *Only a little while longer and then I'll quit all this and lead a normal life.*

I listened to that little self-deceptive mantra for over a decade while working in the industry. When that one tired, there were others to take its place.

I can quit when I want to.

I am in control.

I am just an empowered woman.

I am doing people a service.

They were all lies.

Occasionally, the need to blow off steam would rise, and I would go out to different bars on a night off just to escape. One evening, the girls and I decided to visit another club, and after ordering my usual cranberry and Southern Comfort — the "Scarlett O'Hara" — I glanced across the room and saw a guy talking to a group of friends. He was from South America, at least 6'3", and suddenly he was walking over to me, introducing himself in Spanish. Unfortunately, I didn't actually speak Spanish. I was in the process of picking up a few words here and there but wasn't able to have a full conversation with anyone yet. He picked up on that pretty quickly and immediately enlisted the help of one of his friends, conveniently equipped with a Spanish-English pocket dictionary, who began translating for us. He told me he worked at a nearby bar and that I should come by and visit him sometime.

"Sí," I told him with a grin; and then, through our translator, "I'll swing by on my next day off."

When the day came, some girlfriends and I took a cab to the bar and were stunned when we stepped out of the car onto the curb of what looked like a castle. Stone steps led up to a massive wooden door that swung open into a foyer and the entrance.

I was accosted by so many new sights and sounds. The room was cavernous, techno music pounded at your temples, and lights swirled around the room. The stone steps leading up to the dance floor throbbed and vibrated; the bartenders, flipping bottles with a mastery I had never seen, were a show in themselves. Glass bottles spinning through the air, refracting light across the room, made it look like a circus going on — only until you walked into the main room, where there actually *was* one going on.

Soaring twenty feet above the dance floor performance art was happening on the stage. In that churning sea of music, light, sensation, and dense crowds, I was able to lose myself. Floating between multiple bars, with no shortage of men to buy me drinks, it felt like a place I could disappear from the world.

That Spanish-speaking bartender was there too, and we quickly began a tumultuous "on and off again" relationship. Most of the time, we would drink too much and then rage at each other with loud voices, cursing each other in languages we didn't understand. Soon, management in my hotel wasn't thrilled to see him because they knew loud arguments, slammed doors, and yelling in the hallways followed close behind. One of my club managers stayed in a room a few doors down from me and asked me if I understood what the bartender was saying to me. When I told him I had no idea, he said that he had never heard such horrendous insults thrown at a woman and that I should immediately walk away from that relationship. But it simply became another addiction.

Not that I needed another one.

My alcoholism was still at an all-time high then a bartender introduced a drink to me called "The Mopet." The concept was simple — shot glass, half tequila, half Sprite. The bartender would pour it, cover it with their hand or a towel, and then slam it down onto the counter, fizzing up the Sprite for you to shoot it fast. My tradition once arriving at the bar was typically three mopets in a row. My drinking had gotten so bad that a night out usually involved throwing up twice just so that I could keep drinking. It should have been another warning light that something was terribly wrong, but who was really paying attention?

Physically, I was a mess, often falling down double flights of stairs at my favorite bar. Emotionally, I was even worse. I was so angry and I was taking out my anger on other people. One night I threw a bottle across the bar to hit the mirrors behind it shattering it everywhere; I was entirely out of control. At some point, whether in Spanish or English, we finally decided to go our separate ways before someone got seriously hurt.

Chapter 10

Vida de la Muerte

IT WAS BACK TO the daily grind at the club. However, one day a group of regulars asked some of us to spend the weekend with them at a posh house on the coast. We unthinkingly hopped in the car with them and drove over three hours to Acapulco. The place did not disappoint — a palatial layout, exquisite marble staircases, and a beautiful outdoor pool. The guys left to play golf but told us to get ready to go out later that night.

Like any good house guests, we started drinking from the house bar, and wouldn't you know it when it was time to go, we were thoroughly trashed. We finally made our way to the club door and our "hosts" came out and ended up telling the doorman they didn't know us and to send us away. Undaunted, we explored all the other bars on the Acapulco strip and eventually made our way back to the house late that night. I had gotten thoroughly drunk but had also become seriously angry. In part, it was because the guys had turned us away, but it welled up a deeper feeling of abandonment that I had been dragging around with me for a long time — and which had been fully triggered through the experience. Unhinged and drunk, I found myself swimming in the pool in the middle of a lightning storm, yelling at God. I dared him, if He was there at all, to just take me out with a lightning bolt. He, like everyone else, had abandoned me, so why not just get it over with?

I woke up the following day naked on a couch. Embarrassed and furious, I just wanted to get back to the city. The guys called a cab to get us home, and I locked myself into my hotel room for a few days to try and sort through the mess of my life and figure out what might need to change in order to love myself again.

I didn't yet realize that toxic, dysfunctional situations had become the norm for me. A deep longing for love and inclusion had propelled me out of a relationship with an abusive husband and straight into the arms of a workplace where I experienced physical and mental abuse every single day. At the time, it seemed like my only option, and yet, it was chipping away at my self-worth, my sense of value, and any sense of purpose in life. My grand plan of escape had simply become another prison.

Eventually, I paid off my debt to the club, received my passport back, and could come and go as I pleased. I worked fewer hours and tried to focus on building a life outside of the club but I couldn't shake my addictions. I was routinely drinking as much as I could endure in an effort to dull the pain, shame and confusion that I was experiencing. I had begun to think I deserved the physical, mental, and sexual abuse I received. Somehow this was all *my* fault and I knew it. I was developing an unspoken hatred in my soul for myself, coupled with a distrust of anyone around me — but I masked it completely. The people in my circle had no idea what was going on inside my mind and my heart. I began relying on the alternate persona I had created for myself — "Lauren" — and would flip her on like a light switch when I couldn't handle the thought of myself anymore. She was all smiles, always sweet, always giving, always loving.

But old habits die hard. And you can't escape yourself. My own confidence and value as a person was determined by how much money I brought in or didn't bring in during my work shifts. It left me in a state of confusion always seeking validation from others but the weight of insecurity fueled even more crushing addictions.

One night I went on a huge bender, hunting for cocaine at all costs. I hailed a cab and began searching the streets for a dealer. I asked the driver to take me to dangerous sections of the city, scanning for anyone who might be able to sell me drugs. The driver told me he knew of a place and took me to an abandoned building where, indeed, I found a dealer. I asked the cab driver to wait for me and then passed by the battered, graffiti-plastered walls, seeking out the only source of light in the building — a dim lamp where the dealer sat. I paid cash and started doing lines of cocaine alone.

After getting my fill, I thanked him and went to the cab outside where my driver was waiting. With cocaine now boiling through my body, I yammered incessantly to the driver, demanding that he take me to a club. After driving for a few minutes, he pulled off onto a side street, which immediately drew a startled yell from me in the backseat. Obviously he was going the wrong way! But it turns out, he knew precisely where he was going; he had alerted some local policemen that he had a high, blonde American girl in the backseat. As he pulled to a stop, they came over to the car and swung open the door. Fear stabbed at my heart and my blood pressure started to rise. They did not look like friendly police officers.

Suddenly, with no way to escape, strange men were hovering over me and one of them grabbed me and held me down. The scene started to blur and, mercifully, I passed out.

By the end of the night, all four men had raped and beaten me, although intentionally avoiding marking my face. They stole my jewelry, threw me out of the car onto the side of a deserted road, and left me for dead. When morning came so did the pain. The angry black and blue evidence of the night before on my body was everywhere, but these bruises were not badges. Since I was already constantly bruised from nights at the club, I knew no one would believe what had happened. I picked the gravel out of my knees and lumbered onto my feet. I stumbled at first, then broke out into a crisp walk with a newfound determination. Something had to change. I was going to die if *something* didn't change. Finally, after walking to a more populated area, I was able to locate someone to give me a ride back to my hotel.

I locked myself in for a couple of weeks. I hadn't been paying my bill, and I knew if I left, they would lock me out of my room. While I didn't actually have *much* to lose, I was afraid to lose everything again after working so hard to build a life for myself. So I waited. I cried. I wasn't sure what to do. Contacting family wasn't an option, so there was only one person I knew who had the money, and perhaps the willingness, to pay my hotel bill and get me out of this situation.

After the bruises had faded I placed a call to David to see if he could bail me out again. I told him through tears that I had to pay my hotel bill, or I would lose everything, and by the end of the conversation, he assured me he was getting on a plane to come to me. Less than 24 hours later, he walked into the hotel lobby, paid my bill, and then knocked on my hotel door. I didn't let him know about the assault. I didn't want him to know such violation had occurred. I was so ashamed believing that it was my fault and I didn't want someone to agree with my assessment. I opened the door and felt a wave of relief.

I was undone; I had never been so thankful.

He graciously spent the next day with me, but I proceeded to drink myself into oblivion. I was working through the trauma of the rape and keeping it a secret from him and tried to block it out. I planned a fun event dining at a rooftop restaurant, with all the lights of Mexico City spread out beautifully before us. I ordered my favorite shrimp and avocado cocktail from the bar, along with a fifth of vodka and I looked at him thinking my heart would burst. Once again, we were at a hotel, me staring at him knowing that nothing could ever happen between us.

After he left, I finally found rock bottom. Unable to manage my life anymore, I called a friend who sent someone from a 12-step group to pick me up and take me to my very first Alcoholics Anonymous meeting.

I was finally ready for change — really.

I was done with being abused and I knew that I had to stop the addictions as a starting point.

On July 15, 1996, I stepped into my very first AA meeting. I wore a baseball cap, no makeup and cried the entire time. When the people around me shared, I finally felt like I had been seen and known.

I sat in two meetings a day for the first 90 days, walking to one and catching a cab to the other.

Whatever it takes.

Even if it was going to take complete immersion in order to change my heart and my mind, I was finally going to break the cycle of addiction.

Chapter 11

Martha Stewart of Mexico

THERE'S A SAYING IN 12-step meetings: "Take the cotton out of your ears and put it in your mouth."

The not-so-subtle idea behind it is that if you're new, then your own thinking got you to the place you are now. So listen to people who are further along in the journey and keep your mouth shut about your ideas, period. That small bit of wisdom has served me repeatedly throughout my life.

When you find yourself around people who are further along in a journey than you, default to listening to what they have to say. If you see something in them — perhaps it's freedom, recovery, or just a higher satisfaction with life — they can share their experiences and learnings with you, but only if you're paying attention.

In recovery, I listened.

It took two meetings a day early on in my sobriety because I knew I needed to be around people who had figured something out that had beaten me to the ground. It was clear to me that one drink would always be too much because I could never stop at one. There wouldn't be a slow quitting process with me — it was full stop or destruction.

Of course, it's still a gathering of recovering addicts, so nothing will ever go perfectly. It didn't take long before several of the men in the group tried to start "relationships" with me. Unsurprisingly, I dated a couple of them — I may have been alcohol-free, but I was still desperately thirsty for attention and affection. One of the older guys I had connected with took me along on vacation to a small town outside of the city. It was a wonderful place, but it didn't take long to notice that there weren't separate rooms — I was obviously expected to spend the night with him. I went along with it because I was now in a different city and didn't want to be abandoned in a strange place again.

He raped me that night and then had the audacity to tell me I should be grateful to him for having brought me to such a beautiful place and spending money lavishly on our accommodations. When we arrived back in the city the following day, it was clear to me that I needed a different kind of relationship. Perhaps if I just *acted* the way I thought a normal person would act, it would make me *feel* normal.

Thus began my sincere attempt to become the Martha Stewart of Mexico. I began hosting home-cooked meals for everyone. I honestly did love the cooking, but when I fed people, they just seemed happier. It didn't take long for orders to come my way — "Hey, could you bake your pecan pie for us?" It was a wonderful feeling; I was finally wanted for something other than pleasure. I was truly appreciated for something that didn't feel sexualized.

Life started to lead me in unexpected new directions. During this time, I came into contact with some local missionaries. The couple had a combined total of about a dozen children and they invited me to travel downtown with them to feed the homeless. They were genuinely kind people and cared for me in ways that I had not been cared for before. Their treatment of me was irresistible. I began spending more time with them, realizing that relationships could be more than just habitual abuse. They invited me into their home, they cooked meals for me, and they helped me begin to believe my life could be something different. I wanted to be better and I wanted something more. In my time of early sobriety, I met and made some of my closest friends. Even now, we are all scattered across the world, but we continue to stay in touch. Being in a much healthier place, I also took a chance with a new relationship. The guy was nice, good-hearted, and funny; I hoped being in a relationship with him could help me heal. However, it didn't last — I was anxious, depressed, and battling inner demons. It was clear I still wasn't ready for a genuine relationship.

The nightly tensions of life in the club came in sharp contrast with the cooking, dinner parties, feeding the homeless, and spending days each week at the lake with my close friends. The lake was my refuge — a place where I felt invigorated and at rest at the same time. My friend who owned the lake house was a fantastic host and we invited people every weekend to drive the short distance from Mexico City to Tequesquitengo. Beautiful lake houses dotted the hillsides complete with pools, jet skis, and boats. We would arrive, throw on our suits, hop in the boat, and get on the water as fast as we could.

As the day wore on, I would begin cooking some of my famous meals. Fresh ingredients were a breeze to find at local markets and I *loved* cooking for my friends. One of their favorites was always "little chickies," which were cornish hens stuffed with wild rice. And, of course, no meal was complete without whipping up some homemade guacamole, bursting with lime and garlic. As I cooked, I'd put on mini-concerts, singing along with the Indigo Girls and Sarah McLaughlin, popping discs in and out of the CD player on the kitchen island. Looking out the window, seeing the lake, and being surrounded by my loud, fantastic friends always made my heart swell. There was something deeply beautiful and healing about those lake days.

Back in the city, I would work to replicate that experience by cooking constantly for friends and cross-stitching. Being the resident "Martha Stewart" of Mexico City was another attempt to become a different version of myself, hoping that I could forget the lights, fog, and groping hands of men that dominated my nights.

The pull between the two lives pushed my mind to the brink to the point where I wasn't sure that I could go on. A doctor prescribed anti-depressants, and while it did help me stabilize, it didn't solve the underlying problems. My issues went beyond depression and chemical imbalance; the foundations were cracked in a deeper place in my soul.

Suddenly, an opportunity emerged to get out of the country for a while and work at a club in Reykjavík, Iceland. Several of us packed our bags and, once again, I flew off to a land I knew nothing about. My connecting flight took me through Newark, New Jersey, and while roaming through the terminal, I was stopped in my tracks.

There, just past the lines of people milling about, was Jimmie.

Of *all* people, how did he end up in the same international terminal at precisely the time I was walking through?

My heart started to race and tears swam in my eyes. What would he do if he saw me? Would he try to hurt me? Would he try to kill me? I ducked around the corner, hoping he didn't see me, and made a plan to grab the nearest security guard if things went downhill.

Thankfully, he never saw me.

He simply walked down the long terminal without turning around.

I immediately ran to the bathroom and started to sob. Despite the emotional turmoil I had been yanked into, my commitment to the 12 Steps held true, and I stayed clear of a drink. Maintaining my sobriety through the severe anxiety of a close encounter with my past felt like a massive accomplishment. Perhaps I was going to be okay after all.

I found my way to the gate, boarded the plane to Iceland and uttered a genuine prayer to God, asking that I would never have to see Jimmie again.

When we touched down at the small airport in Iceland, I was initially confused. It seemed like the middle of nowhere, with absolutely nothing around. A driver picked us up and we began our long drive into Reykjavík.

The Icelandic country was barren and beautiful — unlike anything I had ever seen.

We were dropped off at the lodging for entertainers and started our shift the next day. Although one of our jobs was selling alcohol, I was sober, so the bartenders made mocktails that looked like real drinks, conveniently charging customers as if they were. Despite the cold of the season, it turned out to be a fun few weeks that included participating in a fashion show for one of the local designers and a feature in a local Icelandic newspaper. I even got to perform some singing sets at the clubs before they transitioned to strip clubs later at night. A month passed by quickly, but before boarding the plane, I rewarded myself with an Icelandic wool blue hat and blue silk scarf — presents to myself to remember the time there.

The change in environment had jarred something loose in my soul. I arrived back in Mexico dissatisfied and uncertain of where I was in life. I began to realize that I wanted out of the industry. I believed I would be happier without it all, but I just couldn't see how I could support myself. In that muddled place, my bestie, Greg, contacted me and asked me if I wanted to visit England with him. He was on scholarship for a prestigious program in London and would be spending extended time there. I jumped at the opportunity to change locations, thinking it might help me dislodge the nagging depression I was mired in. So, for six weeks, I lived in London, England, making rounds to all the tourist spots and falling in love with the culture and people, just as I had upon arrival in Mexico City. We went to every musical possible. We swayed to the tunes of "Dancing Queen" at *Mamma Mia!*, sang the opening notes of *The Lion King*, and fell even deeper in love with one of my favorite musicals, *Les Misérables*.

A college friend of ours was in the cast for *Les Mis* and provided tickets for amazing seats, even taking us backstage after the performance. I distinctly remember walking out on the stage afterward and feeling like it was somehow familiar, as if I was supposed to be there. I started to sing, "I Dreamed a Dream" from the show. It was about a character that had to turn to prostitution in order to support her child. It was a song of regret about how her life had turned out. I knew I didn't want to live my life with regret. My dreams never seeing fruition. Being on stage and singing was something that resonated in my soul. In that moment, it was like a seed of faith was planted in my heart — maybe one day I could use my voice again onstage instead of my body. It was time. I had to make a change.

With so many options for travel, we took a quick trip over to Ireland. I wandered cobblestone streets, ate delicious food, got a small tattoo, and drifted through the Irish countryside and coastlands. The beauty of the rolling green hills elicited an unexpected longing for the green hills of Kentucky. Something inside me leaped at the possibility.

Home.

Could I possibly start over again?

However, when my funds ran low, I decided to fall back on what I knew best. Back in England, I called a dear friend from Mexico who created a spot for me as an adult entertainer in one of the local bars for one night. I donned my sequin dress and a diamond choker, and performed to the best of my ability, seeking the same validation from men in London that had been so reliably poured out on me across the world. But this time, it was different. Somehow, it made me feel lonelier than I had been before.

There in England, during the summer of 2002, was my last show in adult entertainment — I would never again take the stage to take off my clothes.

The trip to London finally came to an end and, before traveling back to Mexico, I stopped in Miami, Florida, for a few days in South Beach with the bestie, followed by a pornography convention happening nearby. Bestie and I stayed at a little boutique hotel in South Beach, and after waving goodbye to him, I caught a cab to the convention in Hollywood, Florida. It was time to get to work. I had previously made the decision to start producing pornography and met up with a friend of mine at the convention hotel to begin scouting for talent. I was convinced I could make better productions than was currently available on the market and was looking to gauge interest from some people embedded in the industry. But the thought already seemed to sour in my heart. Was this *really* what I what I wanted to do? In any case, I was out of money from London so I needed to stay in the hotel room he had booked. There was uncertainty about the next few days, but I forged ahead anyway.

As stood in the hotel lobby, checking in, it was impossible not to notice the frenzy of people looking to buy an experience.

The industry was sex. Toys, costumes, videos, and magazines littered the area. Strippers, models, porn stars, porn consumers, men wanting sex, women wanting money — everyone wanting to be loved.

It was all I ever wanted.

The deep desire that had led me to this place had been the unrelenting ache to be loved by someone. Anyone. I wanted to be protected, treasured, and adored. I wanted someone to calm my fears, tell me everything was going to be okay, and take care of me.

But one issue lingered in my mind. I couldn't escape the nagging thought that I was supposed to be doing something different. Something inside me whispered that I was made for something else, perhaps *anything* else. For a long time, I had not been able to put my finger on what it was, so I had moved forward in the only way I knew.

I suddenly needed to be out of that room. I was making my way through the hotel lobby when a strange thought ambushed my mind:

I could escape.

I could just leave everything.

My heart skipped a beat. My mind argued. *Probably impossible.*

I walked out through the front doors and into the smothering South Florida heat. *Should I even go back to my home in Mexico*? There had to be something beyond the meaningless "success" I had achieved for myself.

My absentminded walk took me alongside one of the most notorious porn actors of all time. He looked happy; why wasn't I? I turned my gaze down a ramp leading up to the hotel and saw a picketer. In his hand was a large, handwritten poster bearing the inscription: "John 3:16."

What in the world does that mean? A prickly teenage memory surfaced about that verse reference: "For God so loved the world..." But it didn't seem to fit. Why all the picketing and judgment to represent a God of love? It made me more confused than ever.

I turned to the crowd nearby and pointed him out. We quickly dove into snide remarks about his life like old pros. The words, "I bet he never gets laid," tumbled out of my mouth.

But as soon as I said it, I felt like I had crossed some strange, unseen line. I knew I shouldn't be making fun of him, and I suddenly felt an unfamiliar pang of guilt. The truth now seemed to be staring *me* down: if I was making fun of him, I was no better than he was; we both were just passing judgment.

It was painful. But it was real. Real was good.

A resolve continued to build in my heart, and the thought came again, this time with stronger force:

I could escape.

That insistent pull toward something different wasn't going away.

This can't be all there is to life. There has to be more.

None of the things I had tried had given me any sense of fulfillment, purpose, or peace. Something about it was all wrong. There was something inside of me clamoring to be released. The juxtaposition of my experiences in London was in stark contrast to the convention swirling all around me. It was my wake-up call. What would it take — what changes would I need to make — so that I could finally become the person I knew I was meant to be?

I turned around, walked back inside, and began to rip out the seams of the plan I had patched together.

A new pattern was taking shape.

It was time to get out of this life.

It began by figuring out how to get out of Miami. When my friend wrapped up his time at the convention and was ready to check out, I told him that I would just hang by the pool until my flight. What I didn't mention was that my flight wasn't for another day and that I was out of money. A cab ride from the hotel to the airport was over $100, which was a significant stretch for my non-existent budget.

So I rolled my huge suitcase down to the pool, sat down on one of the luxurious lounge chairs, and, surrounded by paradise, started to sob. I felt utterly alone. I was ready to change everything, but I was simultaneously exhausted. The crying gave way to sleep, and after a brief nap there on the pool lounger, I gathered my energy. I decided to use my remaining pennies to catch a ride to the cute little hotel in Miami Beach where I had stayed with Bestie a few days before.

The same guy was working the front desk when I arrived, so I explained to him my entire situation.

"I am in dire need of a place to stay for a while until I can get money wired to me and get to the airport. Please,

I'm begging you — is there a room where I could crash for a little while and leave my suitcase until I set up a wire?"

Inexplicably, the man looked at me with genuine compassion and told me that there was a room under construction that was available for me to use. He even let me use his phone to make the call.

An angel in disguise, my friend.

After making a call for someone to wire me money, I walked to a nearby drugstore equipped with Western Union to retrieve the cash. After the walk back to the hotel, I closed the door behind me and caught another nap before calling the cab to the airport.

When I was finally on the way to the airport, there was a fresh strength brewing in my heart.

I am strong. I can do this.

With every step toward Mexico, there was a new resolve building. *Something has to change. I'm not sure how, but I can't continue like this.*

PART THREE

I can never escape from Your Spirit! I can never get away from Your presence!

Psalm 139:7 (NLT)

Chapter 12

A New Kentucky Home

IT WAS TIME TO abandon another life. I thought breaking free of the adult entertainment industry in Mexico would be an uphill battle, but to my surprise, they let me go without a fight. When I informed them of my decision to leave the industry, they told me I had been there long enough and had paid off my debt. At the time, I had dialed back my hours to only a couple of days per week, so it was a win-win for both of us for me to move on. What had seemed impossible was suddenly reality. All I had to do was walk through the open door.

I later heard a story that circus trainers condition elephants at a very young age to stay put by tying them with a rope to a stake in the ground. When they're young, it's enough to hold them, no matter how much they strain against it. By the time they grow up, they have given up the fight; they are conditioned to believe they cannot break away. They could snap the rope with a shrug, but they never even try.

That was me.

I had been held by a sliver of rope to an entire lifestyle and industry, never realizing I could have broken free at any time.

But now, the rope was cut and I was free.

I had made a decision that my body was no longer for sale and I could finally live the life that I wanted. With that decision, it threw everything off-kilter in my situation. My current relationship had already begun to crumble because I had no idea how to be with someone in a non-toxic way. It became clear that I needed some space — time to get away and think through how to straighten out my new life.

The invitation to Kentucky came at just the right time.

Bestie asked if I would visit him back in Kentucky to hear him sing at a wedding, so I packed enough for a two-week stay and hopped on a flight. There was a wide open door at my mom's house, and after a few days, things started to roll into focus.

I was not going back to Mexico.

After all my travels and all the pain, I was home. If I was going to find a place to work on myself and find peace, why not where my roots began in Kentucky?

It was time for a radical shift. I dumped all my plans, all my ideas, all my thoughts, and messaged the man I was living with to tell him that I wouldn't be back. He let me know that he had sensed it was where I was headed and that it would probably be best for everyone if I took the time to sort out my heart and life.

It looked like a brand new life. But the same deeper issues I had wrestled with in Mexico had simply boarded the plane with me. Sobriety had brought enduring freedom, but there were nameless realities warring on the inside - things I would later recognize as self-loathing, shame, and emptiness. But at the time, I was simply looking the part.

I'm fine.

Things just didn't work out in Mexico.

It was just time to come back.

Having decided to stay in Kentucky, I talked to Greg to see if he had space at his house where I could stay while I sorted some things out. He said yes and I moved my few remaining belongings into his house in Lexington. Starting over sounds like a refreshing change — and it was — but I also needed a whole new source of income. I began hunting for jobs - anything I could find. I cleaned houses, babysat for families, worked at a floral shop, and ultimately landed a job at Victoria's Secret in the mall. I worked every hour I could throughout the whole winter season, living off Red Bull just to stay awake. I was tired, but I was employed. I was supporting myself and no longer having to take a stitch of clothing off. The sheer relief was like a tiny ember glowing through the darkness in my inner world.

And then came the invitation to church.

Greg kept nagging me to come to visit his church with him.

Seriously? If I step through the doors, that whole place will burst into flames.

I had tried to make some kind of connection with God before. While in London, England, I once walked up to the doors of a church, looking to enter, but the doors were locked tight. It seemed appropriate — I assumed that the damage I had done was so extensive that God had locked me out too.

This time the message was different but still confusing to me.

"God so loved the world He gave His only Son."

But to me, I believed any love from God was going to be conditional on seriously cleaning up your life. If that's what he needed, then fine — I could work hard, clean up, and finally be good enough. Even still, it took several invitations from Greg to wear me down, but in the end, I relented.

The little church seemed different. The entire sermon series was woven around movies, which was interesting to me. I hadn't heard anything like that before — especially not at church. And not just any movies, the one they had been focusing on recently was *Lord Of The Rings.*

And since we're talking church, it's confession time. I was a *diehard* Lord of the Rings fan. Not kidding: my name is literally in the final credits of the extended version of *The Fellowship of the Ring* as a charter member of the Lord of the Rings Fan Club. Yes, I even have a card to prove it.

So, yes, I was intrigued by the whole concept, but I had my reservations.

I wonder what these Christians are gonna do with ME?

I was curious how well they could tolerate someone who looked a bit different from them, so I decided to push the limits. I donned my favorite gold leather pants, a black silk shirt, and a black leather jacket. I teased my hair to 80's levels and climbed in Greg's car — it was time to go to church!

We pulled up to a tiny strip mall harboring a few small businesses and surprisingly a church. Not your standard church building. It threw me off a little and suddenly I was a bit nervous.

"Are you sure you're going to a church and not some cult meeting?"

Now that I was there, I didn't actually want to go in.

Wordless anxiety began clawing at me.

I lit a cigarette, took a few very long drags, and stomped it out with my steel-toe boots right there on the sidewalk. This church — or whatever it was — wasn't going to get the best of me. Determined and ready for anything, I walked through the doors.

Immediately, I was greeted by a woman that embodied everything I understood about the idea of a "Christian woman." She was older, sporting a floral print dress with shoulder pads, and wearing absolutely no makeup. My mind reeled. I could never — and will never — be *that*. However, she locked onto me with such focus that I assumed she was about to inform me that I must have walked into the wrong place and needed to leave immediately. But instead, she came up to me and said,

"Hey, are you Greg's friend? Why don't you come and sit with me? I've got a seat for you."

I couldn't believe it. She must have absolutely no idea who I am.

Or did she?

Another wave of anxiety rolled over me. Had Greg told everybody about my past? Smiling through gritted teeth,

I told her I would follow her. We found our seats as the lights dimmed and music started to play. I looked around me. People were raising their hands and singing, and it seemed like everybody knew the words. Thankfully, the lyrics were up on a screen so I could try and mumble along with them, but I kept my hands firmly pinned to my side. The music played on and standing in that dimly lit hall full of singing, tears began streaming down my face.

What is going on?

I couldn't stop it. I kept wiping them away, but they just kept flowing.

At some point, I began looking around, wondering if it was happening to anyone else. It was the strangest thing — I wasn't weeping out loud nor had anything "sad" happened — but the tears didn't seem to respect that at all. They just wouldn't stop.

When the music finally came to an end, I took a few deep breaths and sat down. I actually listened. The message the pastor shared started to make sense of how God could love and accept someone no matter what their past was.

For the first time in a very long time, I was hearing some unexpectedly good news.

CHAPTER 13

WHEN GOD WHISPERS YOUR NAME

THE CHURCH SEEMED GENUINE, but I was still skeptical.

It was time for some testing.

The people who went there seemed happy. Since we were in church, you could even describe it as "joy." So I began floating some personal history their way, specifically my work in the adult entertainment industry.

They didn't flinch.

I kept attending here and there over the next few months. I even got roped into volunteering. Greg was helping them paint the kids' section of the building and invited me to come to help them paint. I reluctantly agreed, thinking that he and I might be the only ones who showed. I was utterly shocked when we pulled into a full parking lot. So many people had given a huge portion of their Saturday to serve. It seemed like the painting work was just an excuse to hang out, talk, and genuinely enjoy each other's company.

The atmosphere of that church felt so pure and life-giving. It cleared my senses, like breathing pure oxygen. I kept gravitating to it without fully realizing what I was doing. At first, it was just a relief to be in a spot where people weren't constantly groping at me. But then I started feeling like it was a genuine sanctuary (ironically, no one in the church ever called the auditorium that) — a place of true *rest.*

Christmas was suddenly on the horizon, and I was excited to be back home with my family. But it wasn't just about family either; there was definitely something different about this Christmas.

At some point, I realized that I was just... *happier.*

I was taking a deeper look at my heart and life. Much more than I had ever remembered doing before. I began asking questions about life and reflecting on how I had ended up on the paths I had taken.

I had the beginnings of some genuine friendships where we shared our hearts, not just drinks, parties, or a lifestyle.

I even started to ask serious questions about Jesus. What did this guy want from me? Most men in my life had always wanted something from me, so what did *he* want?

During the services, I would listen attentively to the words coming from the stage, and I never tired of looking around at people while they were singing songs. Greg's cousin, Barbara, became a friend during that season, and we sat together most of the time. When Barbara was singing, she developed a mesmerizing look on her face — I think it was pure happiness. When we stood to sing during the service, she would stand beside me and lift her hands up to the sky. The first time she did it, I was totally confused and a bit worried.

Is she some kind of weirdo? What's up with her hands? What does that even mean?

In time, it became a bit more routine to see her raise her hands during singing, so I decided to give it a shot myself. I made sure no one was looking and then I turned my hands up so that my palms were face up. I was curious to see how it would feel and was stunned when the floodgates of emotion burst open in me again. It was like touching a live electrical wire somewhere inside. Unnerved, I quickly dropped my hands to my sides, lowered my head, and tried to look casual as we sang along.

I remember one song in particular called "Amazing Love," which I couldn't get through without weeping. It talked about Jesus being rejected and crucified but how He rose again for us. Out of love for us.

I honestly didn't understand what some of it meant, but I couldn't deny that it spoke to my heart in ways that my mind couldn't grasp.

Months passed and I began to piece together what everyone around me seemed to understand: Jesus had been sent for all of us... including me. The well-defended walls I'd built up in my heart and mind started to come down, brick by brick.

However, the only way I knew to respond was to dive headlong into involvement with the church. Surely that was what Jesus wanted in return, right? It was time to do some serious volunteer work. All the people at the church that seemed close to God were volunteering, so wouldn't it help me develop a better relationship with God, too? If that's what could make me a Christian, then I was ready to work the plan.

I volunteered.

And volunteered.

And volunteered.

I even attended a class at the church about "spiritual gifts" that were supposed to help me serve even better. Apparently, everyone had them, and I was desperate to figure out what mine were. It turns out that one of the gifts was making music to God as a way of saying "thank you" and letting other people know what He has done for them. Incredible. I can use my voice as a gift? So I began contemplating joining the singing teams that served during the weekend services. As long as I didn't have to raise my hands, I figured I would be in pretty good shape.

I knew that if I was really going to do this Jesus thing right, I was going to need the appropriate tools, so I decided to hit up a Christian bookstore. While sifting through a shocking variety of Christian gifts, I came across a set of tabs that are meant to be inserted into a Bible to help you in locating the different books and chapters. Yes! It felt like that would be so helpful since I didn't know where anything was in the Bible. Immediately, I snatched those Bible tabs up, convinced that this was going to help me learn. To be clear, I didn't actually *have* a Bible, but I saw the tabs as an investment in the future. One day I *was* going to get a Bible — and I was going to be ready.

When the Easter series arrived that Spring, the focus of the services had turned to the crucifixion and resurrection of Jesus. I knew I had heard some of the content before, but sitting in the services, it felt like it was truly registering for the first time. I was confounded by Jesus' choice to be crucified in place of human beings and take on the punishment for their sin because I had experienced a lot of that sin up close and personal. I had known some folks that deserved what was coming to them — why would Jesus volunteer for that?

But then it started to dawn on me: *I was included.* Instead of giving me what I deserved for the choices I had made that separated me from God, this news about Jesus meant that I could have a relationship with him, and through that, my relationship with God could be restored. Perhaps there *was* hope after all, even for someone like me!

The pastor said, "Next week, I'm going to give everyone an opportunity to accept Jesus as their personal Lord and Savior and ask Him into their hearts." I sat up straight in my chair.

That could be my chance!

I could not believe that something so important had escaped me in the past six months. I had assumed it was all about knowing more about God and Jesus, or even just serving more as a way to gain His good graces, but what if it was really about responding to His invitation that He had already given?

The next week, as I sat in the service, I prayed quietly,

Jesus, if this is my time to give my life to you, please let me know.

It was the first time I had attended both services and it was if God knew I needed to let it all sink in that I was about to change my entire life. Was I ready?

Yes.

As if in response, the pastor spoke from the stage during his sermon,

"You know, I have a friend. Let's call her Sandi. And she asked me what her life would be like if she gave her life to Jesus, and I told her that her life would be incredible, amazing, and filled with worship."

And my, how the tears started to flow.

In my heart, I knew it was for me; he had said my name! It was almost all I needed to hear.

Jesus, I will give my life to you in the next service. I would like to be there with my friends when I do it, and if this is really meant for me, please say my name again.

When the next service began, my friends, Greg and Barbara, sat on either side of me. During the sermon, the pastor was revisiting his points from before and got to the same point: "I have a friend, let's call her Sandi...."

I knew that it was my time.

One of the passages from the Bible they spoke about that day was from Revelation:

> *"Here I am! I stand at the door and knock. If anyone hears my voice and opens the door, I will come in..."* (Revelation 3:20 NLT).

It was the picture I needed to bring all the puzzle pieces together for me. Although I had been getting to know

Jesus for a while, my experience had been analogous to opening the front door of my heart, peeking out, and then quickly closing the door without letting Jesus in, all the while marveling about how amazing it all was.

But this time was different. When the invitation was given for me to give my life to Christ, I bowed my head and repeated words from the pastor that was on stage.

Yes, I believe Jesus died on the cross for my sin and that He is the son of God and was sent to save me.

Yes, I ask You for forgiveness of all of my sins —
past, present, and future — because You took
them all on yourself.
Yes, I receive the gift of Your forgiveness.
Yes, I ask You to live in my heart to lead my
life because I have made a mess of leading my own life.

In my mind, a clear image formed. It was me, kicking open the door of my heart from the inside and inviting Jesus in. As we embraced in the doorway, the door closed, but this time, He was inside with me. That deep, sad, lonely, empty place I had nursed for years was suddenly filled; I was embracing him, and He was embracing me.

Sitting there in the small church auditorium, I opened my eyes. Something was different. Perhaps everything was different. The room seemed full of light, and I quickly inhaled — my first breath on the other side of truly knowing Jesus. It was like breathing for the very first time.

I turned to Barbara and said to her in a small whisper,

"Barbara, I opened the door to my heart all the way and let Him in."

We cried and we celebrated. She let me know that all Heaven was celebrating, that God himself was celebrating that I had finally come home, and that He could redeem everything in my past, present, and future.

It was April 27, 2003, approximately 12:10 p.m.

I had given my life to Jesus.

How precious are Your thoughts
about me, O God.
They cannot be numbered!
can't even count them;
they outnumber the grains of sand!

Psalm 139:17-18 (NLT)

CHAPTER 14

AD IN HD

IT WASN'T ALL "HAPPIER ever after." After giving my life to Christ, things didn't automatically get better. There were still consequences to my own sin patterns. There were things I needed to unlearn. There were also things I needed to learn for the first time too — and I was ready.

Shortly after coming to Christ, Barbara came over to the house where I was staying with my bestie and handed me a beautiful little box. She said, "I know you have the tabs because you've talked about them, so I'm sure you have a Bible, but just in case you don't, I got you one today.'

I opened up the box and found a beautiful leather-bound Bible complete with gold edging; it was all mine! Barbara had written on the inside "For opening the door all the way." I spent that entire day sticking those tabs in that Bible and knowing that I was going to be studying Something that was eternal, life-giving, and heart-altering.

Five days later during one of our conversations, Barbara suggested that I audition for the worship team. I was familiar with performing instrumental auditions, but I had never done a singing audition. However, I found my courage and agreed to go for it. I grabbed the lyrics to the only song I knew, "Amazing Love," and signed up for the audition later that day. I was nervous when I arrived, but I was convinced it was something I was supposed to do. I walked into the little auditorium, handed the worship leader a piece of paper with all my information on it, and climbed the 3 steps to the stage.

1.

Oh my gosh, what am I doing?

2.

It's okay. You'll be fine...

3.

Ok, God, if you want me to.

I placed the lyrics on the black metal music stand and asked to start in a low key since I was an alto. The song began and as I started singing, I also began weeping. I couldn't control the tears. All the lyrics were true: "It's is a joy to honor God"

Despite the fact that the audition leaders really didn't get to hear much singing as I croaked out the words through tears, I made the team! I'm sure for a long time they just turned my mic volume down and let me stand onstage, crying and singing off-key throughout the entire worship set.

Baptism was another one of those initial steps that seemed like an important one to take. I had seen people baptized and knew that I had not been baptized since giving my life to Christ, so it probably needed to be on my agenda. As I pursued that step, something critical about the role of baptism became really clear to me. Baptism wasn't salvation. It had often seemed to be treated that way by people I had known and was often the implicit message of the church of my youth. What I came to understand was that baptism was an outward response to what had already happened inside you. The act of baptism was meant to be a step of obedience to Christ to let people know publicly what had gone on in private.

And so, I got baptized. As I emerged from the water, dripping wet, I was wrapped in a towel, and stepped back into the choir loft, finishing the day out worshiping God from a deep place of gratitude.

Although I now had the Bible to go with the tabs, I really hadn't read much of it yet. However, I did recall that someone was once asked to take off their shoes because they were on holy ground. Our church was the place where I had encountered God so clearly, so I started running around barefoot every time I was there because it was holy ground to me.

I didn't just worship with my feet though. I sang and sang, leading people in worship every single weekend I could. I volunteered for anything and everything, showing up for every possible meeting. I even managed to score a role duplicating sermons on cassette tapes.

Yes. Cassette tapes.

These were pre-streaming days and CD duplication was a step beyond the fledgling church budget. If someone couldn't be there in person or just needed a second listen, I was there to make sure they had their opportunity. I'd stand barefoot making duplicates onto little cassette tapes believing I was for sure changing the world.

Not long after, I joined a small group of women at the church and we met every week on Sunday night. The whole concept was a little strange at first, but it was refreshing and encouraging to spend time with people who had experienced challenges in their own life — not necessarily challenges like mine — but challenges nonetheless. I found it fascinating to be around "normal people" in this little group. I was surrounded by women of all ages who were seeking Jesus, having beautiful conversations about how their heart was, and sharing what they were thinking and doing. I distinctly recall sitting back one day and thinking,

How is this my life now? It's surprisingly gorgeous.

The leader of the group became a close friend and I began sharing my heart with her. I remember sitting on the side of the tub in her bathroom, finally admitting the unspoken suspicion that I was far too broken to ever be in a healthy or meaningful relationship again. I sobbed out my fears to her, "I don't know of any man who would want me after everything that has happened to me and that I've done."

Undaunted, she said, "Let's pray about it." And so we began a prayer process, asking God that if I was to be in another relationship, He would be preparing that person to understand what I had been through and love me just like Jesus would.

For me, the initial years of knowing Jesus was a relearning of everything in life, but especially how to be around people in a new way; a way of servant leadership, genuine love, and passion for Jesus in a world that needs so much hope. Despite the challenges I was facing, I knew I was different and I wanted people to know why. I crafted an email sharing what Jesus had done in my life and sent it out to an array of people from my past. Although I didn't have very many responses (which was expected and understandable), I wanted the honest truth to be out there for anyone willing to listen. I wanted to encourage them and offer the same hope that was given to me — no matter where they are in life, Jesus loves them and is there for them. I was truly eager to share the truth of what had happened in my heart and my life after I had given my life to Christ.

A year or so after following Jesus, I was approached by one of the church leaders and asked if I would be willing to tell my story during one of our church services. It was like the chance I was waiting for! Sitting down with a woman who would later become a truly great friend, Jennifer, we began talking through my story. Her role was to help me learn how to tell my story in a succinct way that would fit well into the service that was planned. After praying that God would guide us, she turned me to and said, "Okay, tell me a little bit about your story."

Two hours later, with tears running down my face, I wrapped it up. With genuine love and compassion, Jennifer gave me a hug, looked me in the eye, and said, "Thank you so much for sharing that. God has done such an incredible work in your life. Now, we need to get that down to 7 minutes."

I erupted into laughter and it was contagious. When we were eventually able to collect ourselves, I took a deep breath and looked at Jennifer, and said, "Okay. I believe we can do this." And, sure enough, the next morning as

I shared my story for the very first time in public, it was indeed 7 minutes long. On the dot. God was gracious to me, as well as all the people listening. In fact, a close relative gave her life to Christ that very same day.

In time, I ended up becoming roommates with two amazing ladies from church that had known Jesus since childhood and had sincerely walked out what it meant to love Jesus and people. It was refreshing to watch them and discover how they responded to different situations in their life because they had such a wealth of knowledge of Jesus. They graciously welcomed me into a little room with a twin bed, which mostly was just for sleeping because I spent almost every waking hour at the church.

As I grew in my faith, I began to sense that the path ahead would lead me to seminary because I wanted to learn as much as I could about God, the Bible, and how to live out His mission in the world. Surprisingly, when I spoke to my pastor about it, he foo-foo'ed the idea, assuring me that I could teach and preach without a degree. While he was right, it left me with a strange dissonance, because I felt like I had disobeyed what I had heard from God. In retrospect, it was my first indicator of something fishy; something I couldn't quite put my finger on. But I was a new believer; surely I just had a lot more to learn, right?

Instead of seminary, I was offered a job working at the church as the secretary, later moving over to a ministry assistant position. With my new job, I was eager to share about Jesus and wanted to take the opportunity to talk to anyone I could. Even though I had whittled my story down to a concise 7 minutes, I was still nervous about what to say if someone honestly wanted to talk with me about God. So one day I prayed that Jesus would just bring someone to me who had questions and that I could share with them about what He could do in their lives.

Less than five minutes after praying that prayer, I walked to the bathroom, followed by a girl who asked me to tell her about Jesus. I'm not making this up! Friend, sometimes all you have to do is ask Him to help you out when you're not really sure what to say next.

If I needed any further convincing, I found it through a phone call to the church office from someone who had dialed the wrong number. When I greeted the caller, he identified himself as Bill. Bill was quite talkative and soon I discovered that he was also known as "Wild Bill" and he had accidentally dialed our church, thinking he was calling his daughter's phone. After just chatting for a few moments, Wild Bill turned the conversation in a direction I wasn't expecting.

"I feel like it can't be a coincidence that I called a church. I've been thinking about that and whether or not I should start going to church again," he said.

Stunned by this revelation, I began encouraging him to seek out a local church and asking him if would be willing to share a little bit more about his past encounters with church.

Instead, the voice over the phone asked, "Why don't you explain to me some of the differences between different religions?"

What Wild Bill didn't know is that Jesus had already been priming me for this moment. The previous Sunday, our pastor had taught a sermon on that *exact* topic – all the different kinds of religions and how they differ from each other, especially Christianity. So I whipped out my trusty note card and proceeded to share the news with Wild Bill. Toward the end of my "sermon," I made clear that a relationship with God is possible through trusting Jesus by giving your life over to Him and receiving the forgiveness He offers.

Wild Bill was full of surprises. After a momentary pause, he said, "You know what? That's exactly what I wanna do. I want to give my life to Christ."

"Bill, I can help you with that right now. We can do this over the phone."

In that instant, old Wild Bill gave his life to Christ and became a new creation. "Wrong number," indeed! Emboldened by that experience, I knew that there was nothing more in my life that I wanted to do than help people understand who Jesus is and who He could be for them.

There were also course corrections that God began introducing into my life along the way. Toxic relationships had become the norm in my world so it was astounding when I began to see genuine healthy relationships developing around me. The power of Christ-centered relationships began to have a lifting effect on my heart, mind, and even my behavior.

When my friend, Justin, and his girlfriend, Courtney, began dating, I got to watch the whole thing from early dating to marriage. Along the way, they invited people to give them good counsel, they invested time in having the right conversations, and they consistently treated each other with respect and love. It was genuinely inspiring to me and began fueling a desire in my own heart to develop a God-honoring relationship. I was even invited to be a part of Courtney's wedding shower and a guest at their wedding, giving me an up-close look at a whole new kind of relationship.

At that time in my life, I didn't really have a dress appropriate for a wedding, so I borrowed one from a friend of mine. To be clear, my wardrobe choices were still heavily influenced by my past, which meant I walked in with an extremely low-cut dress. I walked into these sweet people's wedding looking like I just came off the stage as Lauren St. James. I felt a tinge of embarrassment and shame, but it was the only dress that was available to me and I hoped no one would mind. In the characteristically gracious and non-judgmental atmosphere of our church, no one said anything to me, of course. But inwardly, I sensed the Holy Spirit tapping me on the shoulder to say, *You don't have to feel shame for this, but can we raise the neckline on your clothing from now on?*

There was something so sweet and gentle about that; no shame, no condemnation — not a command, just a question mark. And the response that came out of my heart was surprising even to me — *Yes! Yes, I want to be honoring with my body now. I don't want my entire body out there for people to see every day.* I was actually happy to agree.

No one at church had told me to change how I dressed, but they trusted that the Holy Spirit would tell me if change was needed and He did. He used the lifting power of a God-honoring community around me, along with the "still, small voice" rooted in my heart, to continue changing and transforming the places in me that were being restored.

That transformation wasn't just for my benefit either. God was transforming the shame of my past into a place of redemption and rescue for others. As the church grew and more people came, we decided to launch a new ministry called "The Mat," which served as a recovery community for people with a variety of issues and struggles. As someone who was in active recovery from alcoholism and drug issues, I jumped at the opportunity to continue the journey toward freedom in community. Even more, I was asked to help lead in the meetings on the worship team. My dear friend, Helen, was spearheading the initiative and perceived that our issue-specific groups needed to begin each meeting by focusing on God more than their issue. Worship not only became an avenue of freedom for the attendees, but it was also another thread of redemption in my own life. Here I was, taking the stage again, but rather than seeking adoration for myself, I was actively pointing others toward hope and restoration in Christ.

After attending The Mat for over a year while still struggling with a private pornography addiction, I approached Helen for help. I was eager to find someone who could sponsor me through this recovery process and asked her if we could explore creating a group for other women who also struggled with pornography as well as other forms of sexual and relationship addiction. With Helen's guidance, we identified a sponsor (an incredible woman and a priceless influence in my life) and began to move forward with the idea for a group. My sponsor began walking me through some material focused on female sex addiction and pornography addiction with immediate results. The reality of what Jesus was doing in my heart and mind, combined with the power of doing the work together in community, began breaking the viselike grip of these issues. As I began to experience deeper healing and freedom, I could scarcely wait for other women to experience the same.

All the same, starting that group felt incredibly vulnerable and I wasn't sure if anyone would show up. But God surprised me. During our first meeting, 16 women came. And the surprises just kept coming. What began that night eventually grew to regular gatherings with over 200 women attending through the first year — all seeking Jesus and finding healing.

During that time, our little church had started to grow so quickly that we rapidly outgrew the strip mall location that housed the church and began looking for a bigger space. Not long after, a new building with plenty of elbow room became available and we orchestrated a move into the new venue. The very last service that happened at the original location — the "holy ground" I had so revered in my first days of knowing Jesus — turned out to be The Mat's weekly meeting. Funnily enough, the electricity had already been cut off, but it didn't seem to dim the sound or power of our worship. Without a microphone,

I helped lead out in an acoustic worship set and we sang heartfelt praises to God. I will never forget the flickering candlelight reflecting off the tear-stained faces of my friends as we poured out love and honor for the One who had led us into freedom and recovery, and was leading us into a new chapter.

With the evidence of Jesus' redemption so palpable, I began thinking about the women that I worked with in the clubs. Was it possible to help them understand the love that's available to them? That question was too big to ignore, so I launched a nonprofit with the sole aim of letting women know they are loved no matter what their profession was.

God had more surprises in store, too. Over the next few years, I was awed by how God used our little ministry to impact the lives of so many women. Fueled by stories of redemption and healing, the grassroots organization expanded to multiple cities. In a stunning reversal, I was given the opportunity to train nearly 100 organizations throughout the United States on how to love and care for men and women who work in the sex industry.

What had been a pattern of darkness, shame, and brokenness in my life was being transformed into an artistic collage of hope, redemption, and freedom.

Chapter 15

Becoming a Savage

DESPITE THE NEW LIFE I was experiencing on so many fronts — I was heavily involved in an intensive leadership development program, leading worship, leading recovery groups, leading and coaching people on how to have effective life groups, and more — there was one thing I couldn't quite rouse my hopes for: family.

I didn't know if it was possible for a man in my life to love me. It was early on in the journey of God's redeeming work in my life, and the idea that He could redeem relationships hadn't quite taken hold in my heart and mind. Even though I was convinced God loved me, I knew men all too well and I knew just how fallible they were. It didn't seem realistic to think that someone could look beyond my past and the persona I had created in order to work in adult entertainment. God knew who I really was, but it seemed completely unlikely for any man to ever see it.

In time, I began to believe that a relationship might not be in my future. The few dating experiences I had were good, but things just never seemed to work out. It was saddening to me, but I tried not to let the weight of it settle on my heart. However, there were times when the dam would break and the unspoken grief would spill out.

I remember sitting on the edge of a bathtub again at the house of a friend when I spilled my thoughts out.

What kind of mother would I ever be to a child?

With tenderness and love, she responded to me, "But look, you're a mother of so many already. You lead so many people. You have helped so many people understand who Jesus is and who He is to them. You're a mother of many!"

It was true and I was grateful. But just as true, there was an undeniable gap in my life; a gap that I had created through my choices and my past; a gap that no man was going to be able to fill.

And then Tim Savage walked into church.

I happened to be sitting on the front row of a recovery service — one of our open share meetings where we would pass the mic around the room and people would share about their life and although Tim wasn't new to recovery meetings, he was new to being at one in a church. So when the mic came around to him, he launched into his story in full graphic detail, punctuating it with the most colorful language ever heard inside the walls of that church.

He was impossible not to notice.

I leaned over to a friend of mine and asked about this fiery, raw new guy. There was a wildness to Tim from the get-go. He spoke from the heart and pulled no punches. His story resonated with me and I was impressed with his brutal honesty.

However, that story is his to tell, and I'm praying he writes that book one of these days.

While he made an impression, we were truly just acquaintances at first, not really even friends. I thought he was handsome and charming, but I kept my distance. But even from a distance, I paid attention. We found ourselves serving together on one of the church's volunteer teams and I watched how he handled different obstacles and circumstances that were emerging in his life.

At the time I was heavily involved in our church's singles ministry, which included a multitude of social events. The annual Halloween party was coming up and after significant deliberation, I decided to dress up as a princess, even though I didn't feel like one. That costume took on a significance I didn't really intend. I was in an ongoing struggle with my singleness, wrestling with God over whether I could be whole as a single person. Would it be enough just to be loved by Him; to be treasured as His princess? I remember staring at that princess dress prior to the party and being driven to the floor in tears, surrendering my heart to him in trust.

After mopping up, I made my way to the Halloween party, and after a series of conversations with friends, found myself standing next to Tim. At one point, while we were standing next to each other, talking with friends, our elbows touched. Both of us realized it and neither of us moved a muscle.

What is going on?

We stood there forever, chattering on with other people as they came by, just letting our elbows touch.

It was electric.

Although the "Elbow Incident" contributed to a growing sense of connection, it was serving together that actually gave us our first opportunity for an ongoing conversation, granted it was via text. What started as scheduling requests and then syncing up on video shoots for our creative team, became a running text thread back and forth. Even during a church service, we would find ourselves texting with each other, and then, interestingly, during a sermon about marriage, we were suddenly asking different kinds of questions and sensing sparks. He asked me if I wanted to grab dinner after an upcoming video shoot and I agreed.

When we finally ended up at dinner, we were having a great, lighthearted time together, when a mutual friend of ours happened to walk by and decided to sit down with us.

"Hey, what's going on here you two? Are you on a date?" he said with a sly grin.

"No, no, no," we cried out in unison. "No, no, no. Just talking."

After dinner, Tim walked me into my car and, in characteristic fashion for both of us, we decided to have a very fast-paced, aggressive, business-like conversation about the state of our relationship. It was like a Shark Tank DTR.

"Do you like me?" I fired at him.

"I'm not sure," he responds.

"Do you like me?" he counters.

"Yes."

It leaped out of my mouth as a point of fact. I had no hesitation.

The questions continued.

Do you want a family?

Do you want children?

Can you accept my past?

It was straightforward and blunt. It was refreshing and freeing. I realized that this was an unabashedly wild, barbaric man, whose heart was being transformed by Jesus, but not domesticated. His personality was large and loud — maybe even bigger than mine— and it struck me,

We are going to make a great couple.

Later that night he texted me back that, yes, indeed - he liked me.

Afterward, on our first "official" date, we decided to make it memorable, so I opted for an elegant evening dress and spent the late afternoon getting ready at a friend's house. He picked me up like we were heading to the homecoming dance and took me to one of our favorite restaurants. We enjoyed the food, we talked incessantly, and we laughed hard. There was just an edge of awkwardness, like dancing with a new partner, but it was clear there was chemistry. Something was beginning.

Dating was bound to be a spectacle because neither Tim nor I are quiet people.

We quickly became the couple you would roll your eyes at.

We wore matching sweaters to Christmas parties and gazed into each other's eyes forever.

We worshiped hard, we challenged each other in new ways, and we let this new Jesus life saturate our relationship.

While I fully enjoyed each season of our relationship, I consciously chose to not run too far ahead in my own mind. One of the ingredients of relationship sabotage I couldn't ever seem to resist was the tendency to start planning out a wedding after the first week of dating someone. Not a smart way to go.

With Tim, I was not going to do things the same.

When eventually it became clear that there might be more to this relationship than dating, we drew people we loved and trusted into the conversation. It was suggested that we take three days to not speak to each other and fast to determine if this relationship was from the Lord.

While I wish I could tell you that my immediate reaction was to break into worship and start praying with hands lifted high, my actual reaction was a little different.

I cussed like a sailor.

We had become somewhat socially entwined, so fasting from speaking with Tim was worse for me than three days with no food.

Point made.

We trusted the people who loved us and went for it. Each of us spent time listening to God and sensed an openness to continue exploring where our relationship could go. As a way of marking that special time and committing to not taking everything into our own hands, we wrote a covenant for ourselves, outlining our expectations about how our relationship would work.

Things in life were starting to take shape. I began seeing a future as a wife, possibly a mother, and serving in the local church. But as amazing as this new dating adventure with Tim was, it was increasingly impossible to ignore that something was off in the rest of my life.

I had been on staff at church for a few years and I was thoroughly exhausted. At one of our leadership retreats, typically a highlight moment of connection with God, I sat down and gave voice to what was brewing inside, tearfully writing out everything that was filling up my time. I knew that working 80 hours per week was not what God had intended for my life. However, I was caught in a deepening cycle of craving acceptance from my bosses and coming to grips with the reality that life was being drained away instead of overflowing out of me.

After I finished writing, I sought out my friend, Barbara, and shared all of it with her. After examining my list, she looked back at me with tears in her eyes.

"You're right. This is entirely off-kilter."

When I left the retreat and arrived back at the church that evening, I sat down with my boss and told her that I needed to step away from my job at the church. I promised I would raise up leaders to take over some of my responsibilities and would continue to volunteer. A two-year process would begin that night, as I slowly transitioned my roles to new people. I knew it was the right direction, even if it wasn't well-received by many of the people involved.

The whole experience seemed to highlight the increasing sense that something was just *off*. Periodically, I would overhear things that were espoused by the leadership of our church and privately question whether they were scriptural. However, I didn't want to incur the label of someone who was choosing disunity with our church leadership, so I generally kept my mouth shut. But something festered. The unrelenting drive to continue growing, to make the church bigger, or to create bigger spectacles was resulting in too much pressure on everyone. I knew that being part of a healthy community was one of the strongest ways I had been able to walk out healing from my past but my healthy community was starting to feel toxic.

As Tim and I continued dating, our relationship itself became a source of contention. When gathering together for church-related meetings, Tim and I were taken aside and asked to sit separately from each other. It was odd: if he was the person I was spending my life with, shouldn't we be in it together?

It should have been another giant red flag waving at us, but somehow, it was easy to ignore.

And time flies.

Suddenly, a year had gone by as an "official couple." We were having such a good time, I barely noticed 365 days had passed. I let Tim plan a fitting celebration of our first anniversary and expected to be surprised.

I was.

He picked me up and we drove around to all of the places that had meant something to us in the past year. Special moments here, special moments there, and toward the end of the night, we ended up at our church. When we arrived, the place was bustling with practices for Sunday services, so I tried to keep a low profile. This was our first anniversary date and it wasn't about sharing it with other people; I just wanted to be with Tim.

As we walked around the church, I was stunned by the different memories that had come to characterize our life together — important conversations, moments when friends or family members had given their life to Christ, and turning points in our leadership journeys. We took the route that passed through the sweeping front atrium, rimmed with a towering wall of glass windows, overlooking the front doors of the church. He had rose petals scattered across the floor, flanked by a table with our pictures on it.

Suddenly, Tim was on one knee next to me, asking me to be his wife.

What a surprise!

It was the *best* of surprises.

I was shocked, delighted, grateful, overwhelmed, and ecstatic all at once. I had no idea that was going to be the night.

The answer was a resounding "Yes!"

The word was barely out of my mouth when friends started streaming in from all across the church to meet us there and celebrate our brand-new engagement.

I knew Tim had a surprise in store that night, but I totally underestimated him. Not only did he propose, but he decided to orchestrate an instantaneous engagement party.

My first phone call was to my mother. It turns out that she was in on the surprise too. Tim had already made a special visit to her home to ask for my hand in marriage. Classic gentleman!

The next morning, I woke up with a ring on my finger. I'm glad it was there because it was hard to believe it was all really happening.

I am engaged to Tim Savage.

I thought I had to be approaching my happiness limit, but the journey toward marriage kept raising the ceiling. After all this time, after all this waiting, after so many disappointments — it turns out there was a man that I was made for and our lives were about to merge together. I couldn't wait to be Mrs. Savage.

There was also this fun business of planning a wedding! Searching for dresses (only the perfect one will do!), asking my friends to be bridesmaids, and actually doing the work of preparing for a lifetime of marriage, not just a ceremony.

True to form, the wedding was an epic production. We chose the historic Kentucky Theater in downtown Lexington with the hopes of filling an auditorium with hundreds in attendance. We printed off invites onto business cards that we passed out at the clubs across town and invited people in off the street. The wedding party was a mere 11 bridesmaids and 11 groomsmen squeezed onto the stage, and the ceremony we created led our friends through a variety of music and worship, a celebration of communion, someone sharing the gospel, and an opportunity for anyone to give their lives to Christ by the end of the service. The reception was a magnificent blur of dancing, music, laughter, and beautiful, encouraging words from friends, before heading over to our new home together as a married couple.

The next morning we drove off to our honeymoon in St. Simon's Islands off the coast of Georgia. We explored the local beach, enjoyed the sun, and savored just being together. Our hearts were so full and we couldn't believe that we were going to spend our lives together. The healing work that God had done in both of our hearts was astounding.

The first year of marriage darted past - a similar pace to that first of year dating. In short order, we were having our next Shark Tank conversation — this time about kids. The time seemed like it was right and we were giddy with the thought that we could have a little mini-Savage running around in the near future. I downloaded a fertility tracking app onto my phone and waited with eager expectation. One morning, I checked on the app and a pink ribbon popped up — a free reminder to do a breast examination.

Ok, I'm 40 years old and going to be someone's mom soon. I should probably start doing this.

I took my left hand and casually placed it over the right side of my chest.

Lump.

That can't be right.

Lump.

This isn't happening.

Lump.

Tears welled up in my eyes and fear stabbed at my heart.

Doctor. I need to call my doctor.

What began as a phone call turned into a blur of next steps.

Are we seriously talking about cancer?

We were newlyweds.

We were just beginning to try for a baby.

Cancer didn't seem to care.

Chapter 16

Tell Your Husband

November 17, 2011.

The phone rang.

"I don't have great news for you — it's cancer."

Stunned. Livid. Denial.

This cannot be part of my story. Hasn't enough already happened to me?

We had prayed faith-filled prayers. We had believed God for His intervention. My family, close friends, and I were sure this was a benign mass — *not* cancer. But the voice on the other line was unmistakable.

Stunned. Heartbroken. Grief-stricken.

The thread of relationship with God that had been weaving in my life suddenly pulled taught and was tested. Was He going to be real and present enough to navigate me through cancer? My conversations with God were genuine and honest, but this was a different level.

Strangely enough, one of the first fleeting thoughts I had was,

Thank goodness I won't have to volunteer as much now.

That should have been another warning light, but was swallowed up by the reality of cancer. The next thought was more on point:

Ok. It's time for a "come to Jesus" meeting with Jesus.

My life in those first few days read like some of those real, raw, slightly uncomfortable psalms from the Bible. On one hand, I was inconsolable and upset. On the other, I was worshiping God and praising Him for His goodness. I put my full weight on the truth that He is constant and He doesn't change. I took verses like Romans 8:28 to the bank:

"We know that in all things God works for the good of those who love him, who have been called according to his purpose." (Romans 8:28 NIV)

It didn't seem like it could be true in this situation, but the more I poured out my heart to God, the more things began to come into focus.

God's love was present in how I even found the lump. If I hadn't been using the app, I wouldn't have found the evidence of cancer when I did.

On November 16th, 2011, I finished a series of testing that included over 60 mammogram images, and a needle biopsy in 3 separate places. For two of the biopsies the large needle collapsed cysts. For the third, a large mass, it didn't. I looked at the doctor who inserted the needle and asked her, "What do I tell my husband?" She said, "Tell your husband you have cancer."

I couldn't believe it. I didn't want to believe it. That mass hadn't been tested yet. I needed concrete answers. I moved into the room with a cancer nurse navigator, and asked her, "What do I tell my husband?" She told me to wait until the test results came back in order to give a definite answer. That I wouldn't know for sure until the next day. To just let him know there is a possibility that is was just a mass, but to be able to receive the call in a place I was comfortable talking or receiving any news.

The next day I was out with Tim running errands and our car died. I was not happy. Nothing was going right. We called a local rental car company to pick us up and take us to their office so we could rent a car until ours was fixed.

In the midst of that car ride, with my husband and the rental agent in the front seat, as I sat fuming in the back – my phone rang. I answered even though she said to be in a quiet place. I was positive it wasn't cancer.

"Yes, Hello?"

"Mrs. Savage, I don't have good news."

It was cancer.

I wasn't ready to pour out my grief with the rental car agent.

But the silent tears started to flow. Tim turned around and looked at me as I nodded my head.

I don't remember anything else the nurse said except the date and time of my next appointment that would turn into scores of appointments.

God's love was present in the availability of medical treatment and then surgery. The surgeon I worked with was encouraging and talented. They helped devise a treatment plan with me and successfully performed the lumpectomy surgery I needed to address the presence and spread of cancer.

At each moment, I could either choose to trust God and step into the challenging unknowns that lay ahead, or I could do it on my own and live in the constant grip of fear. It wasn't just a "once and for all" choice either — it was constantly being tested and renewed.

For example, 30 hours after the initial surgery, I trusted God to give me the strength to speak at a women's event in downtown Lexington, encouraging them to take risky steps and live the fullest life they could. I seriously doubt I looked like the picture of health, but I hoped it gave them a picture of God's power in our weakness. I propped myself up on a podium and poured out my heart, trusting God to speak through my voice. I truly believe He did. That didn't change the fact that I needed a serious nap and extended downtime after that event, but it was worth it.

During recovery, I started talking with God about what my next risky step might be. After all, I was a public speaker, often challenging others to take their step, so what was mine?

The growing sense of dissonance continued to grow in my mind.

Something feels off in the church I love.

One day while there, I walked by a painted wall mural, featuring an expansive, growing tree, overlayed with the words from Acts 2:42-47 (NIV):

> *They devoted themselves to the apostles' teaching and to fellowship, to the breaking of bread and to prayer. Everyone was filled with awe at the many wonders and signs performed by the apostles. All the believers were together and had everything in common. They sold property and possessions to give to anyone who had need. Every day they continued to meet together in the temple courts. They broke bread in their homes and ate together with glad and sincere hearts, praising God and enjoying the favor of all the people. And the Lord added to their number daily those who were being saved.*

I loved that passage and had walked around on the holy ground of our church, feeling like it was happening all around me. But as I stared at those words, it felt less true. Rather than a growing, multiplying, living organism, it felt like something was stunted. Looking back, I can see that it was gradually becoming more focused on the leadership of the church and how well volunteers were serving *leadership* as an expression of their devotion to Jesus. The God stuff was getting tangled up with ambition and it created an unspoken competition around who was in the "inner circles". I had the thought - this affects all of us and hundreds of volunteers. Those that were laying down their lives to serve Jesus. I didn't want that to be my spirit. I didn't want people to be led by me that way. It began a recalibration and healing work by God in my heart that took a few years to untangle. I'm not perfect by any means but I am understanding more each day what true servanthood leadership is supposed to look like in the church.

Interestingly, our church was a member of a denomination that originated from a missionary spirit. Its entire history was built on the "sending" of people out into the world, in obedience to Jesus' Great Commission in Matthew 28:16-20. But in an ironic twist, we weren't sending anyone out. We were just amassing an impressive collection of strong leaders who loved the mission, and at times, veered dangerously close to idolizing those who were leading us. There were parts of me that wanted the accolades. Wanted the praise and the titles from man. Pride from being on the inside. I didn't have appropriate boundaries and I was just learning how to set them. I saw that I was putting man's voice above the voice of God and knew something in my heart and mind had to shift.

As I stood in front of that tree, I knew that sending was a part of the plan, so I started praying,

"Lord, should I be a part of this or do you have something else in mind?"

But my very next choice was what to do with the news from the surgery.

There was incredibly good news:

The cancer is out and all the margins of tissue around it are clear.

Yes!

Lymph node biopsy came back clear.

Yes!

But this was a particular type of cancer — triple negative — which has a high recurrence rate. Even though the cancer hadn't spread, there was still going to be chemotherapy as a preventative measure.

Are you kidding me?

Yet even in that, there were moments of reprieve. I was to receive the "T+C" chemo treatment, which is quite different from the dreaded "A" chemo treatment (commonly referred to as "the red devil"). While any chemo treatment is no joke, it was a place to be grateful. What's more, I was graciously spared the radiation treatment that so many other brave cancer patients are forced to endure.

In light of that fact, I had the unique opportunity to undergo a double mastectomy and reconstruction during the same surgery. Instead of chemo, mastectomy, radiation, and reconstruction over a period of a year, this treatment looked like a 6 month journey with a more hopeful conclusion.

Do you trust God because He makes things easier for you? No. You just trust God, regardless of the outcome. However, as this journey through cancer was knit together, these moments of grace became opportunities for me to store up gratitude and build trust in God's presence, working all things together for good.

Chemo Treatment, Day 1.

I wake up early. Can't sleep.

It's grey and cold outside.

I suit up in a shirt gifted to me by my friend, Helen, and donned a leather wristband sent to me by Holly — a pastor in California and cancer overcomer herself. The wristband stared back at me, reminding me that I am a warrior and to be courageous in this battle.

When I arrive at the doctor's office, they take an obscene amount of time explaining what was about to happen. It's important, I know. They need to diligently explain what to expect over the next few weeks.

Dry mouth, tiredness, digestion problems, nausea, extremely low white blood count levels, my fingernails may deteriorate, dry skin, loss of appetite, flu-like symptoms, and hair loss beginning in about 10 days.

It truly is important information. They give me a printed version of the whole thing, knowing that someone about to receive chemo for the first time has about an 8-second memory span. I kept that packet on a bedside table throughout the entire experience; what a lifesaver.

None of that changes the fact that it's like finally summoning the courage to climb to the top of the high dive, creeping out to the edge, and then having someone stop you, saying, "Now, wait a moment so I can tell you what to expect."

But, finally, it was time.

I have the gift of having my husband, Tim, with me. Not just the first time. He says he will be there every single time. He sits by my side and holds my hand through every doctor's visit, every treatment. So many people walk through this arduous process alone. I had my best friend in the world with me every step of the way.

Another gift of grace.

We walk back to a small pod where the chemo treatment is administered and they explain to me that the first time I receive the medication they will have to ensure I don't have an allergic reaction. It means Chemo Treatment #1 is going to take longer than any of the others. It's almost as if they are giving you more time to absorb the reality of what is going on.

Needle time. I really don't like needles.

I had already been through several rounds of needles at this point in my medical treatment. Almost every nurse had been challenged to get a needle into my veins. It wasn't their fault — they were amazing at what they did and always kind to me — but apparently my veins were unusually strong.

I brace myself.

They aim what feels like a spear-sized needle into the large vein on my hand.

No good.

The pain starts to escalate as they try again. Tears start to roll down my face.

In a few moments, not only do I need a break, but everyone does.

I need a fifteen-minute breather and at just the right time a cancer survivor I know, Amanda, walks in. She had been diagnosed with cancer just a few weeks before me and had already started her treatment process. She just happened to be there at the same office.

Another gift of grace.

We speak for a few moments, grab each other's hands, and all pray together.

Let's try to get this needle into my vein again.

Success!

I'm dosed up with fluids and Benadryl in case I have an allergic reaction. If you've never had Benadryl pumped straight into your blood system, it's quite an experience. This stuff *burns*.

As the IV pumps, it's a strange feeling to be burning on the inside but increasingly chilled at the same time. A member of the team slides a heating pad around my arm and slowly the fluids are warming. (I loved that heating pad. Not only did it keep me warm during those treatments, but it also turned out to be my secret weapon against my super-strong veins. Heating my arm before the needle was inserted made the whole process much less painful.)

What Benadryl lacks in pleasantries it makes up for in sheer power. I wake up 30 minutes later only to realize that I am going to be here for a long time — *much* longer than anticipated. We strike up conversations with everyone nearby, we watch TV, I scroll through Facebook on my phone. Time seems to inch by. I fall asleep again.

What began at 7:30 a.m. finally wraps up around 5:00 p.m. I've literally put in a full day's work to receive my first treatment. They hand me a prescription for nausea meds and encourage me to take one even if I think I might get sick. Preemptive strike.

The nausea meds work. Throughout all my chemo treatments, I only got sick one time.

Ten days later, exactly when they told me it would, my hair starts falling out.

It was Tim's birthday.

The next day, hair is practically drifting off my head. As we process and pray through that, it feels like God is speaking to us: "Every hair you lose is one step further into My plan for your life."

So, we decided to go ahead and shave my head.

Let's *run* into God's plan for our lives.

There are side effects with chemo.

Heartburn. Uncomfortable dry skin. Flu-like symptoms. Fatigue.

My immune system is sidelined so there's a real risk to being in large crowds. And things like hugging people are generally frowned upon.

I decide to risk it.

A gala for our non-profit has been on the calendar for weeks — I can't miss it. I speak at the event and even shake one person's hands.

Then I'm sick for a week.

But it was worth it.

The rounds of chemo come and go. It becomes a routine of sorts and I'm committed to working the plan.

July 10, 2012.

Surgery day. The chemo treatments are done so now it's time for the next step.

Tim and I are in the car early, driving over to the hospital. The chemo had done its work and I have been recuperating. There's some hair already growing back and my strength is returning. My fingernails are still detached from the skin, all the way down to the quick. It won't be permanent, they tell me, and they're right.

We get to the hospital and I'm clothed in a standard gown. We went through the plan with the doctors again.

6 hours.

Mastectomy and reconstruction, all in one go.

We pray, remembering that there are so many friends and family members praying for us right now, and invite God to partner with this surgery in the healing work.

A short while later, the team is sliding me from a wheeled stretcher to the cold metal table in surgery, a gigantic light overhead staring me down.

The meds do their job and I don't recall a thing until hours later when I wake up.

I'm going to share some details of what happened, in case you or someone you love ever have to go through this. Some of it is pretty graphic, so if you get queasy, feel free to skip down the next few paragraphs to "When I woke up." But I know some of you like the medical write-up, so here goes...

First, quick reminder: my surgery was not typical. There were several factors about my body structure that made it possible to have a double mastectomy and reconstruction in the same surgery. For example, before I turned 30, while still working in the sex industry, I opted for breast implants. At the time of my mastectomy, I was a size E, so the amount of skin they had to work with it made immediate reconstruction possible. Not your average situation.

Now: the double mastectomy.

The incisions for the surgery typically go from under the arm straight across the chest bone on each breast. For me, because of the amount of tissue, my incisions were more akin to a breast reduction surgery — think the shape of an anchor, from between the breasts and down then around the base. Once the incisions are made, they completely remove all the breast tissue — one of the most time-consuming parts of the procedure.

The skin reshaping process cuts away a third of the skin and removes the areola and nipple. The rationale is that these areas have ducts, which makes them prime candidates for cancer growth. Removal is just the safest way to go.

Once the tissue is removed, the plastic surgeon is up.

My implants were over the muscle but the muscle had to be separated from underneath to install new implants. Implants come in a variety of sizes, so I had given my surgeon full permission to make the best call in the moment as she evaluated my body size and structure.

Believe it or not, at this point, the surgical team sat me up to make sure everything was in its "natural placement" (thanks, gravity), then laid me back down. They installed drainage tubes into the surgical site and then stitched me back up. For the next two weeks I would empty and measure the fluid that came out of the tubes on each side as it gathered in little plastic receptacles that were held in a pocket of my surgical bra, until the tubes were removed by the plastic surgeon.

When I woke up, Tim was beside me, just as he was the whole time. Coming out of anesthesia was tough and the next two days were difficult.

The pain was real.

To be fair, it wasn't just from the incisions. I somehow ended up with a nerve pinch in my back from the surgical table. It was enough pain to keep people concerned and they kept me in the hospital for an extra day to observe my recovery.

It created issues in my ability to breathe, so they issued me a plastic device to make sure I could and that my lungs were exercising. For the first weeks, I was using that gadget a few times every day. I would sleep propped up with a pillow over my chest so my cats wouldn't jump on me.

After Day 4, I was done with pain meds, and the healing process went remarkably well.

Another gift of grace.

Cancer wasn't easy. It wasn't what I would have picked. But in everything, God really was in the midst of it, working things together for my good.

Even still, it was a fight, and some days it felt like rounds of boxing that seemed to go on forever. As time went on, one thing became increasingly clear, solid, and anchoring:

April 27, 2003, was the day I had given my life to Jesus and that was the day that the battle was already won.

The words God spoke to a young man, Joshua, who was facing down a long series of fights, held as true for me as they did for him.

> *"This is my command—be strong and courageous! Do not be afraid or discouraged. For the Lord your God is with you wherever you go."* (Joshua 1:9 NLT)

Notice what that *isn't.*

It is not a suggestion from God.

It is a command.

A command to be courageous, even in the face of formidable obstacles. He promises that He is with us; He is the Protector. Our part is to trust Him that He really makes all things work together for good.

The courage that had sustained us through the ordeal was called for at the end, too.

The pathology report.

We took a deep breath and prayed.

No cancer.

No cancer.

No cancer!

It was a moment to celebrate, and it was also a cue we had been waiting for. God had been faithful to carry us through all this, and now we knew it was time to grip tighter to His hand and take a risky step forward.

Throughout the cancer treatment and surgery process, Jesus had been prepping me for the next big risk, setting me apart and purifying me in ways that only going through this could. We had been praying and God had been opening some interesting doors of relationship and opportunity in the most unlikely of places.

Miami Beach was calling our name.

Not for a vacation, but for ministry.

The pattern God was weaving into this moment was undeniable. The last time I was in Miami was for a porn convention. I had left there with my heart stirred for change and the determination to begin a new kind of life. That journey had led me to Jesus and now following him had led me back to this moment — but this time with a mission. His ability to redeem anything was simultaneously shocking and comforting to me.

If He can do this in my life, what else might He have in store for the people of Miami?

On Week 3 after my surgery, it was clear the prayers I prayed in front of the painted Acts 2 tree were answered: *we* were the ones being sent. After speaking to our leadership team, we could tell everyone wasn't on the same page with that call. Some were upset with our decision to leave, while some were very encouraging of our willingness to step out at trust God. Looking back, it's easier to see some of the stress fractures that were emerging among the church leaders, leading to the dissonance. Although we knew it was a decision that didn't make everyone happy, we trusted that God was with us, so we packed our bags and headed for Miami -- our next big risk... We wanted an outpost for Jesus set up in South Beach.

It was time to be courageous.

Chapter 17

Un Cortadito Por Favor

"BIENVENIDO A MIAMI," WAS the refrain in our hearts and on the stereo as we rolled down the highway, brimming with dreams and a growing vision for the work we were to do in Miami. We were elated about the adventure ahead of us. We made our way from Kentucky to South Beach, Miami, believing that God had a role for us to play in the lives of other people who wanted to love and follow Jesus in the same way we did. We didn't know what role but trusted Jesus to fill in the details as we went along.

One morning during my daily devotions, I had an unexpectedly powerful encounter with God, where I felt Him whisper to my heart something like:

"The best way you can show women that there is life after trauma, after all the hurt and betrayal, is to live your life beyond your past. Let them know and see there is more purpose to your life than building something good, even a non-profit, around something that happened to you in your past. You are more than just your past. You are more than even the redemption of your past. You have a glorious future and you are a new creation."

While the expansion of the organization and its impact had been awe-inspiring, it was suddenly clear to me that we needed to send out all the groups in different cities and states to become their own nonprofits or ministries. In order to "send out" these mission-minded people, it was time for me to step away from the helm of the non-profit and plunge into the next great adventure that God had for us.

Even now, I am humbled and grateful for the dedication of hundreds of volunteers from across the country that resonated with the mission of serving women who worked in the industry. Those dear people were the ones who ensured that women knew there was someone they could reach out to if they needed anything, even if it was just for a listening ear over a cup of coffee. There's so much more to say about my non-profit experience and working with various denominations, churches, and organizations throughout the country and abroad, but that's a whole separate book for another time.

Convinced that I was ready to take the necessary steps to move on from that wonderful season of non-profit leadership, I strolled over to our favorite Cuban coffee shop. Despite having only been there a short time, I already had my regular — a *cortadito.* So with a glimmer in my eye and a strong jolt of caffeine, it was time for a new day.

I don't know what you think of when you hear "Miami," but at that point in my life, this is what it conjured for me: sweltering heat, sandy beaches, virgin mojitos, Cuban coffee, and beef empanadas. That this was about to be *home* was a living, breathing *dream.* I had been invited to speak at some local churches in the area earlier in the year and had begun strong friendships, so not only were we getting tropical weather, beaches, and exquisite food, but also a new extended family.

Upon our arrival, we immediately went to work. We started thinking and dreaming about what kind of ministry we wanted to build. We wanted to create a place where people would be accepted and loved exactly where they are because *we* had needed a place like that. A decade ago we had been incredibly lost in life, begging for anyone to love us. Convinced that this kind of unconditional love was central to the ministry we were to lead, we initiated small get-togethers around the city, first on Lincoln Road and then at a sweet little French café on Española Way.

Let me be clear though, Miami is not all wonderful ocean air and gorgeous beaches. We quickly discovered the underlying poverty and rampant addiction that marked the transient population of South Beach. We knew this was going to take more than just our own efforts, so we began organizing prayer walks and partnering with other organizations, pulling all sorts of people in to minister in South Beach.

As Tim and I were getting ready for bed one night, a strange, unbidden thought entered my mind.

You should Google your ex-husband's name.

Perplexed, I looked at Tim and said, "Tim, I heard the strangest thing just now, like a whisper to Google my ex-husband's name. Do you think that would be okay?"

Without missing a beat, he said, "If you heard it, do it."

So I Googled my ex-husband's name. The man who was the source of untold trauma in my life, had introduced me to multiple addictions, and that I had fought to escape from in my early twenties.

The first search result was an obituary.

I discovered that Jimmie had died a few years before. Despite the pain that he had caused me, my prayer had been that he would discover Christ just as I had before he died. Uncertain of what had transpired in his spiritual life and eager to involve my husband in the decision, I decided to ask Tim if he was okay if I reached out to the funeral officiant to find out more. With compassion and grace, he agreed.

Making a call to the woman who had performed by ex-husband's funeral ranks up there on the list of "experiences you'd never expect to have."

"Hi, this is Sandi Savage. Could you please tell me about my ex-husband's life before he passed away?"

Her answer was immediate and warm.

"Yes, absolutely. He started going to church a couple of years before he passed and even sang in the choir. He was still an alcoholic, which is what killed him in the end. He had cirrhosis of the liver but he was well-loved by many and seemed to be at peace."

"Could you tell me where his grave is?"

"Yes."

He had been buried in a cemetery in North Carolina. Still uncertain of all the reasons why, I looked at Tim and said, "I think I have to go to the site." He agreed and I began a road trip to see the grave of my ex-husband. Once I found his gravesite, I sat down beside it and spent the next hour, overcome by weeping.

When I was finally able to talk, I spoke to Jimmie. I told him the truth — of how he had harmed me and how I had lived in fear of him. But I also told him about Jesus and what He had done for me, and perhaps, what He had done for both of us. I poured out my heart, raw and honest, at that grave, and when I finally came to the end of what I needed to say, I knew the only thing left was to forgive him. Not because he deserved it, but because none of us deserve it and yet God forgives us anyway. Who was I to withhold that from him — even the one who had terrorized me? With tears coursing down my cheeks, I whispered to Jimmie that he was forgiven. A few moments later, I stood up, a bit shaky, but different. Something had truly shifted. I wasn't free of him because he had died; I was only truly free from him once I had forgiven him.

I didn't realize how important being at that grave would be. There are still times, even to this day, when if I see someone that looks like him, my heart stops. I have to take a deep breath, count to ten, blink my eyes a couple of times, and tell myself, *No, that is not him. I have seen where he is buried and he's no longer here.* Even more importantly, I remind myself that I have forgiven him and I have moved on.

When the day finally arrived to launch our first church service, it felt like a miracle that any of it was even happening, much less that we were getting to be a part of it. We chose a bar downtown to be the site of our first church service and opened our doors to 123 people who joined us. The undeniable highlight of the day was the surprising turn in the life of a sweet girl who had wandered in off the street. After hearing the message, experiencing the community, and talking with us, she became the first person we had the honor of leading to Christ that night. By the end of the night, we were spent and deliriously happy, traveling home with tears in our eyes and gratitude in our hearts that we had front-row seats to a miracle.

After a few weeks of continued ministry, the weather shifted and Miami lay in the path of a hurricane. In the aftermath, we made a decision to hold services in a different place, so we approached a friend of ours about using her tattoo shop as a potential place to host church. She loved it. We held services early in the morning, before the shop opened up, but after the bars started to close. Our vision was that people could leave the bar, come in, have a cup of coffee, and hear about the love of Jesus for themselves. People came and the little church grew.

Despite the joy and gratitude we were experiencing while leading the church, the realities of leadership were formidable. We discovered so many things that we actually weren't prepared or trained for, and the mental and emotional weight began to exert pressure on my heart and mind exposing new places I needed to heal and learn.

In addition to the responsibilities of leading the church, we had another full-time job as chief fundraisers of the whole operation. The unrelenting financial burden started to bear down on my soul, and I grew increasingly fearful that we were going to be evicted from our home. Soon, we would not be able to pay our astronomical Miami rent and so we started selling everything. At one point, when we had run out of things to sell, I moved all of our belongings out of our condo and into a storage unit, just in case we were evicted and needed to relocate immediately. Every day was a "wait and see" on pins and needles.

I had also started receiving hate mail in my inbox because I was a woman preaching the gospel. I didn't understand why as the church I had given my life to Jesus in had two female teaching pastors. I started asking the question, "Is it not normal to have women preaching?" I started to question my voice and my calling. It created confusion in my heart and mind about the next steps I needed to take.

While we are courageous, we also know that God gives grace to the humble, so Tim and I had a heart-to-heart about the future. We admitted to ourselves that we weren't completely equipped to continue running the church ourselves. Coupled with the fact I was unsure of my calling to preach it landed me in a place of feeling defeated. So we cried out to God for an answer and with humility came grace. We had become friends with the leadership of a larger church in the Miami area and they were looking for a location in the South Beach area. After a few conversations, we made the choice for our church to become one of their church sites scattered across the city.

Still reeling from the extended emotional toll, we moved to a small bungalow on the back of a friend's property. We leaned into community in the form of some partners we had developed through ministry, but I began fighting battles with depression and post-traumatic stress disorder. Our income was barely keeping us afloat and I was trading website services for the rent we owed. Old painful memories began resurfacing and dominating my thoughts and feelings: the ache and panic of having nothing in Mexico, living on people's couches, always living hand-to-mouth. It felt like something was slowly imploding inside; an anxiety that I thought I would never experience again.

The burning fuse finally detonated one morning when we woke up to an invasion of ants in our bungalow. I don't mean a few here or there; I mean a nightmarish movie scene where ants of all sizes and kinds are literally streaming in through the cracks and crevices of our home.

Something snapped in me and I cried out to Tim in desperation, "Tim, you have to get me out of here. I can't live like this anymore!"

And so he did.

We had the conversations we needed to have and I started doing the work to seek healing for my mind and heart. Asking God to show me the root of where trauma was coming from and to show me next steps. I talked a lot with trusted friends and after some time we even sketched out a plan to begin work on building a business again.

Although it had gone far differently than we dreamed, we realized that we had accomplished what we had sensed God calling us toward in Miami. The church was never our possession, it was God's house. There was now an outpost, alive and active, in South Beach, helping people discover and walk with Jesus. We could entrust it all to the capable, called people that God had brought there and step forward into the next He had for us.

Chapter 18

The Beach and Bar Songs

FOLLOWING THE ADVENTURE IN Miami, we found ourselves back in Kentucky once again. Although we were grateful to be back among friends, there was a sad note of loss in coming back. The church where Tim and I had met, where we had spent so much of our life together, was finally forced to reckon with the mounting dysfunction that I had sensed under the surface before leaving for Miami. A spectacular crash occurred, leaving a lot of people hurt and angry. While it was ugly for a long time, the church survived and was navigated toward a season of restoration under new leadership. Although we weren't as connected due to our time in Miami, we felt the pain deeply and mourned with others who were wounded. For me, there was gratitude to God for bringing truth to light, but it exposed another layer of betrayal and hurt that I thought I had left behind. Untangling that knot took time, prayer, forgiveness and a willingness to heal.

It took seeing the local church through God's eyes. Made up of flawed people but still worth fighting for. Still His plan and still necessary. That there would be people that mis-represent His name but there are far more people that love Him and want to represent Him well.

The next years I spent learning how to live in the present, finding contentment in the Lord and not people and outside approval, and praying for the church communities I met along the way. The journey toward emotional and mental health is not an overnight trip, and I needed the space, therapy and time to also work on my health. I started losing hair in chunks and my days started to feel like I was walking through molasses. I was afraid cancer had made its return and went down the familiar route of blood testing. We found that living under intense pressure for an extended period of time had nearly taken out my thyroid, resulting in hypothyroidism. My body seemed to understand what my mind was just catching up to — I needed to take care of myself. I knew I had to make space to heal not just my heart but body as well.

The time I took wasn't just physically restorative. I experienced a resurgence of creative and entrepreneurial thoughts again; life started to feel like the world had color seeping back in. Tim's mother taught me to knit and there was something deeply therapeutic about the simple task of working to create with my own hands. The process of knitting helped me regulate embedded anxiety and shift my moods. Soon, picking out yarn — just touching the different textures, soaking in the colors, and enjoying the patterns —was a source of genuine joy again. Not only that, but I had a network of family and old friends all around me. Their love, companionship, and connection kept soothing and healing the broken places inside.

It was truly good to be home.

After a couple of years in Kentucky, Tim's Baltimore-based parents let us know that they had just purchased a home in St. Augustine, Florida, and would be relocating in the not-too-distant future. However, since his mother was still actively working, they couldn't make the move immediately. They weren't thrilled about the prospect of an empty house, so we ended up volunteering to keep the lights on until they were able to permanently relocate.

Once again we packed our things and set our course for Florida with the intention of heading back to Kentucky as soon as Tim's parents arrived. Despite the previous heaviness associated with Florida and the beach, I had walked through a season of recovery and God had been generous in shifting my heart.

The city of St. Augustine was an utter contrast to the experience of Miami. While it has beautiful beaches and great waves to catch, like most of the eastern Florida coast, as the oldest city in the United States, it has a deep history that penetrates every corner of the downtown area. Despite its growth, it maintains a small-town atmosphere and boasts some truly delectable food. It felt like a new country to explore and enjoy, and we dove in. Tim and I would take regular walks along the beach to dream about the future and pray for the future of our family, still believing there was a child in store for us.

One day, driving over the Vilano Beach Bridge, peering across the sunlit expanse of land and sea, I felt a question for God well up from my heart.

Why? Why did you bring us here?

The response came clearly and swiftly.

To heal you.

Already feeling quite restored and healthy, I wasn't quite sure what that meant at the time, but I knew enough to simply trust Him.

Okay, whatever you say, Lord, I'm gonna believe you for it.

Even without the details, I knew I just needed to be faithful to take the next step I knew to take.

One thing that was clear to me was that I needed to search for a community of people who love Jesus. Not only was I a long way from my family and friends in Kentucky, but I also believe we should be in community with other believers.

Let's keep it real. If you have been in a church community for any amount of time, I'm sure you know that church is not perfect. It's an unfortunate side effect of the glaring imperfections in people — you and me included. God is in the midst of all it, but from the New Testament until today, the world has still yet to see an ideal form of the kind unified, loving, life-giving community that Jesus commissioned into existence.

Church had been a mixed bag for me. I have seen and experienced the greatest heartache and betrayal through church, I've been filled to overflowing with joy through church, I've personally witnessed full-on miracles through church, and a little bit of everything else in between. I stood in awe of God as I worshiped and sang on stage, when thousands of people surrendered their hearts to Christ, all in one moment. I've also wrestled with the reality that one of my pastors consistently requested for me to massage his shoulders, beginning when I was a new Christian, and no one seemed to think that was odd. It was only when I started dating Tim that the inappropriateness of that kind of touch occurred to me. Where was Jesus' church in that kind of abuse? Why in the world did no one speak up for me?

In time, here is what I came to understand. The Church is not going to be perfect because God really entrusts it to the hands of flawed people. That being said, we should never tolerate abuse because it's not the heart of God or the plan of Jesus for His community. If you ever find yourself in a toxic, abusive, or manipulative environment calling itself a "church," I truly believe it is right and good to leave. Use your voice and speak the truth to those in authority, and then be content to move on. I have had to do exactly that and I know you can have the strength to do it too. Jesus once told his disciples to "shake the dust from your sandals" and move on when they ran into unexpected difficulty, and I think it's some of the best advice for those who have experienced something similar to what I did.

But — please don't give up on the local church. Jesus isn't giving up on the church. He is fully committed to His people and is forging a family out of all our messes. Don't let the pain of the past rob you of the plan and purpose of God for your life. Don't be a victim of your past.

I was once told that "the local church is the hope of the world," and while I understand the heart and intent behind that statement, I wouldn't say it quite like that. Here's my take:

Jesus is the hope of the world.

Church is one of the ways He has chosen to help us experience life together in all of its messiness and splendor.

While we visited a few churches in the St. Augustine area, I ended up connecting online with a church in Nashville that a friend of mine attended. The co-lead pastor of this church was a woman and her words seem to drip with the substance and power of God's Word, which helped me begin to trust her. Through she and her husband's teaching and my experience of that church community, so many of the hurts from the past were healed. God began to rebuild a sense of trust in my heart for church leadership. Somehow a church in Nashville — The Belonging Company pastored by Alex Seeley and her husband, Henry — became my "home church" and still is to this day. The first time I attended in person I watched her worshipping on the front row, adoring God, instead of working on her talk last minute or rummaging through her notes and it was water to my soul. It taught me so much about trusting God for what He wants to say through you as a speaker and pastor and not only relying on a clever way with words or your own skill.

You'll always find me online, in person when possible, and at the yearly conference kicking off with leadership plus the next few days where we gather from around the world to learn, worship and be in community together. I also have a wonderful church community in the town I live in that I adore. It is important to find your people wherever you are so that you can do life with each other on a regular basis.

Healing from church hurt is possible my friend.

When the time finally arrived for Tim's parents to move down to St. Augustine, we were elated. We were eager to see how they planned to remodel the house and decided to rent a little place on the island while they renovated it to their liking.

While we waited, I found a new desire welling up from within me — I wanted to sing again. God knit me together with an enduring love of music and that passion had been shelved for a long time. I took a chance and started frequenting open mic nights in some of the local bars, singing along with musicians who had become friends. The healing was finding its way into my voice and soul, liberating songs that had been held at bay. For the sheer creative enjoyment of it, I began writing songs and sharing them with whoever wanted to listen.

While the creative side of my mind was flourishing, I was running a business on the side, offering coaching and consulting on business start-ups, website consulting, and non-profit best practices. I even began toying with the idea of owning my own yarn shop! I didn't know if the beach community of St. Augustine would be an ideal market for a retail yarn location, but it was freeing to experiment with the thought. Just to test the waters, I hosted several online classes and had a blast teaching people how to knit online!

It was a lighthearted and fun season, even if it was a bit of a transitional, liminal space. Tim was performing at clubs and I was singing at open mics several times each week. In our free time, we'd head down to our favorite beach on Fourth Street and surf, laugh, and delight in the ocean. Tim's mom and I would visit local fabric shops to pick out fun colors for quilts that we wanted to make. It was an unexpected gift to have Tim's parents right down the street from us during that season of beauty, rest, and adventure.

The day we turned on the TV and heard the news that a massive hurricane was headed toward St. Augustine, it seemed a bit surreal. The idyllic little community and routine that we had forged for ourselves didn't seem due for an interruption, but it was barreling toward us nonetheless.

Since we lived on the island, we battened down the hatches, traveled inland to stay with some friends, and readied ourselves for a storm. It was more frightening than I would have thought, especially after the experiences in Miami. Night after night, the hurricane-force winds and rain seemed to pummel our little beach town. We started wondering if we would actually have a house left when we returned.

When the winds died down, we trekked back across the bridge to the island and, thankfully, found our house was still intact. Many of our friends were not as lucky. The storm surge had generated massive water damage, filling a friend's home with 4 feet of water. Over the next month, we tried to help as many of our friends and neighbors as possible, clearing out their houses and starting the long journey of rebuilding.

But just a few short months later, we were glued to the TV again, in shock. Another hurricane was on its way.

This time we knew the drill. Along with Tim's parents, we all packed up our things and headed inland for a hotel stay to ride out the storm. Overnight during our first night, around 4:00 a.m., there was a sharp knock at the door. A fully-outfitted firefighter was standing there to tell us that the hotel was being evacuated and that we needed to move immediately to the adjacent restaurant on the property.

Minutes later we discovered that while we were sleeping, the hurricane ripped the roof right off the hotel, leaving it uninhabitable. That's how we found ourselves, along with Tim's parents and two cats, at an IHOP booth in the early morning, with no place to go. We sat together, each of us trying to avoid the implications of the obvious question: if the wind was strong enough to blow the roof off of the hotel, could it have blown the roofs off our houses?

After a day at IHOP, the travel restriction was finally lifted for St. Augustine, although the island where we were renting our place was still off-limits. When we finally arrived at Tim's parents' house, we were floored that the house was still standing. In fact, there was no real damage to the place at all.

Meanwhile, we were grappling with reports we were getting from friends in our neighborhood. Water had been at least 1.5 feet deep near our house. Finally, we received photos of our place and were able to breathe a sigh of relief. The water had miraculously stopped at the front door without entering our house. Two hurricanes without damage or flooding. We knew God was being gracious.

As we pitched in to help neighbors and friends in the second clean-up effort, we became aware of a different kind of storm that was impacting my family in Kentucky. People that we loved were hurting and they needed our help. While we were reluctant to say goodbye to our season in St. Augustine, we knew what it was like to weather a storm. It's not the sort of thing to do alone.

For the second time, we departed Florida and headed back to Kentucky, trusting God with our future and family.

It turned out God had both in mind and was about to make good on an old promise.

You made all the delicate, inner parts of my body and knit me together in my mother's womb.

Psalm 139:13 (NLT)

Chapter 19

The Birth of a Savage

After transplanting back to Kentucky, we had some unfinished business. Our family was still missing that child we were waiting for. Cancer had rudely hijacked some of our hopes, but we are Savages and we weren't going to give up on our dream of having a baby.

The doctors had told us that we should create a sizable gap of time between cancer treatments and conception, so we heeded their wise advice. We took the time to pray and prepare our hearts for a new season. When chemotherapy finally registered a few years behind us, we began the process of trying for a baby. At first, we were just a happy couple, enjoying the attempts and eagerly expectant. But every month we tried to get pregnant, each passed without success. As my cramps started each time, the tears flowed. My heart would ache, but I gripped tight to the promises we had sensed from God — we were going to be parents.

But as much fun as trying to get pregnant is, two years of trying is a long time to hold to a promise.

At length, we decided to turn to doctors for help in conceiving. I had no idea at the time that our choice would simultaneously become one of the most challenging and rewarding experiences in our lives.

After gathering input from friends who had successfully gone through IVF, we chose a clinic in New York. My age would have been a factor for most physicians, but this group was different. They were game to try if we were and I was grateful for all the extra encouragement I could get at that point. The clinic hosted an unofficial group on Facebook where those of us going through the process could connect and I started searching through the posts, learning everything I could about what lay ahead. Everyone thinks that perhaps they will be one of the lucky ones; that they will get pregnant on their first try.

We were no different.

Just to give you a small sample of the kind of "luck" required, let me give you a quick overview of what's involved. (I told you before, I know some of you love the medical details, so here goes...)

To warm my body up for my eggs to be retrieved, I was subjected to 19 injections. Yes, *19*. Then, I became a part-time resident at the doctor's office. Ultrasounds were administered every other day to monitor egg development and to gauge the exact timing of the eggs' release.

At a precise moment — like at a specific hour and minute — you get the fun privilege of giving yourself a shot in order to release the eggs for a timed retrieval with the doctor. For the actual procedure, a long needle is inserted into your pelvic area to retrieve the eggs from your body. Thankfully, you are blissfully unconscious under anesthesia for all of it.

The eggs go on a journey to the lab where they are mixed with previously collected sperm and the process of growing embryos begins. Around Day 3, they freeze the embryos for future transfers and you get to pick when you want to transfer them for a potential pregnancy.

But wait, there's more!

Another spread of meds precedes the transfer procedure. Pills, pills, pills. And more injections. When I finally arrived at the clinic, my sides were aching from the shots I had already received. I had been informed that acupuncture would help relax the uterus, reducing cramping, so I submitted to the process immediately preceding the transfer. By contrast, the actual procedure was simple. Guided by ultrasound, the embryo was placed in an optimal location and then began the real labor: the two-week wait. Doctors will tell you that during the initial two weeks, you are "technically" pregnant, but it feels like holding your breath for 330 hours.

So we waited.

Two weeks dragged by.

When the day arrived for the blood pregnancy test, I waited eagerly by my cell phone, filled with hope, expectation, and joy. After all that we had endured and all the time we had patiently waited, I *knew* we were pregnant.

The phone rang.

The nurse calmly let me know we were not pregnant.

Not pregnant?

I believe I cried for a week.

But then it was time to recover and try again.

And try again.

And try again.

After a few more failed transfers, Tim and I were still convinced that we were supposed to be parents. We posted a Facebook video sharing the experience, during which Tim announced through tears, "We have heard that we will have a daughter and her name will be Josephine."

What was that?

This was news to me!

While I knew we had heard from God that we were going to have a daughter, it was on Facebook Live, along with the rest of the world, that I discovered we were going to name our daughter Josephine. But I trusted my husband in his hearing and felt convinced in my spirit as well.

However, after the next failed transfers, I decided to give my body a reprieve. It is extremely taxing to live with the level of hormonal injections needed to make an appropriate environment for an embryo to implant. I had gained a lot of weight, and knew, physically and mentally, I needed to take a pause.

I remembered the little dream of a yarn store that had ignited my heart during our time in St. Augustine and decided to finally open my own little shop in Lexington, Kentucky.

Can I be honest with you? Running a retail location is not for everyone. And it wasn't for me. Although I loved yarn, crafting, and teaching, managing a store didn't reach the same level of passion. Now, I knit for self-care and not as a business. I discovered that returning to speaking, writing, and singing about Jesus and letting people know He can give life-sustaining peace, joy and purpose was a shot of life into my own soul. Even helping people grow and develop their own respective abilities was life-giving to me. Learning and teaching what I had learned to others. A crucial bit of self-knowledge finally came into focus during that season. First, I thrived on projects that needed a kickstart to begin, but also had a clear, definite ending. Second, teaching and writing were rocket fuel for my creativity, passion, and joy levels. I love helping others share their stories of redemption as well. Just walking a path of obedience, doing the next thing He asked me to do, revealed those simple realities about how God knit my being together. Some things just take time and patience.

A few months later, Tim made a visit to his parents at their new home in St. Augustine, Florida, along with his brother and his wife. During an extended conversation with our sister-in-law, Alyssa, she said something that would change the trajectory of our lives.

Tim's mom and dad dismissed themselves from the room and Alyssa turned to Tim and said the words that changed our life.

"Hey, James and I have been talking about it, and we have spoken to your parents and we all agree it would be an amazing plan. Will you let me carry your embryos? I would love to be able to be a gestational carrier for my niece so that she could be born."

Stunned, Tim immediately called me and we prayed about it. We spent extensive time talking to her about how difficult the preparation was for embryo transfers. She was unfazed. She had been paying attention to our trials and was completely ready. More importantly, she had given birth to two healthy boys and had no history of infertility. With hope rising in our hearts, we all decided to say yes to the new plan.

The struggle is real though, friend. The injections were not easier just because she had been pregnant before. The multiple trips to New York to meet regularly with my doctor didn't just magically fit with her schedule. We all felt tested by the difficulties we faced, but when you hear something from God and know in your heart that it's true, you have to hold onto hope.

She had experienced two failed transfers by the end of 2019, so we decided to make one more attempt in March. However, the world was about to change. COVID-19 swept the land and our transfer plans were put on hold.

It was time to wait. Again.

8 months passed.

Almost enough time to birth a baby.

In November 2020, everyone finally felt comfortable enough with all of the protocols in place to travel to the clinic in New York for another transfer.

On November 7, 2020, we transferred an embryo.

I will never forget the doctor looking at us and saying, "I think it's a girl," and then praying with us afterward.

Two challenging weeks later, we again picked up the phone with Alyssa on the other line. My heart was expectant but trusting Jesus in His timing.

"We are *pregnant*!"

Tears again. But this time, tears of gratitude. Tim and I fell to our knees, overwhelmed that we were going to be parents.

10 years had passed while we waited and endured infertility.

A decade of waiting.

But we were finally going to have a baby.

A whole new flurry of doctor's appointments began. Alyssa was based in Cincinnati, so I began regular trips to be with her through each one. Alyssa's baby belly started to show and we finally got to shout to the world that we were going to be parents. The photoshoot included Tim, myself, my sister-in-law, Tim's brother, and their two children — because this was a family undertaking. We wanted the family in the picture announcing the news because it impacted all of us.

Despite the elation of finally being pregnant, the next months were mentally and emotionally draining. While I knew and believed that I was going to become a mom, the presence of my baby in someone else's body, two hours away, extracted a higher toll than I had expected. In an effort to stay present to this little emerging life, Tim and I would record songs and deliver them via an app. Alyssa would then put headphones on her stomach so the baby could hear our voices from the womb.

On the day that we were to find out if we were having a boy or a girl, Tim made the trip with us to the doctor's appointment. The three of us were waiting in the room together, eyes locked on the doctor and our hearts in our throats.

"It's a little baby... girl."

Tears, tears, tears.

We already knew her name and had been waiting for her.

Sweet Josephine was on her way.

Close to the due date Alyssa started having false contractions — not that any of us knew that at the time. We rushed up to Cincinnati in the middle of the night, assuming it was the real deal. However, it turned out to be a great trial run. We nailed our route, spent time talking with nurses who worked the night shift, and toured the hospital so we would know exactly where to go when it was finally time. All the same, we weren't eager to keep commuting to Cincinnati, so Tim leaned over to Alyssa's belly for a little father-daughter talk with Josephine.

"Honey, it's time. It is time for you to come and meet your mother and father."

The next morning, Alyssa began experiencing contractions — serious ones — so we jumped back in the car to make our way up to Cincinnati. When we arrived at the hospital, her labor continued, but it didn't seem to progress toward delivery. They dosed her up with Pitocin to speed things along, and once again, we waited. With time inching along, I opted for a quick break and a nearby lunch. However, when I arrived back at the room, it was like stepping onto a movie set. Huge lights were shining, the doctor was barking orders at nurses, equipment was pulled to the side out and new machines were rushed in.

I made my way over to Alyssa just in time to hear the nurse say,

"It's happening now. Get your gown on!"

What in the world was happening? It seemed like 20 minutes ago we were hours from delivering this baby!

The nurse proceeded to tell me Josephine was slightly tilted in utero. So when they moved Alyssa onto her side Josephine shifted perfectly into position, prompting Alyssa's body to dilate from 3 centimeters to 9 centimeters immediately.

It was time!

They flipped on my gown and I stationed myself next to Alyssa's head with her husband standing close by at her feet; Tim and his mother waited right outside the door.

Push!

Alyssa and Josephine were remarkable partners. Alyssa pushed like a true champion and Josephine responded. They worked so well together that a mere 13 minutes later — which the hospital staff called the fastest delivery in the history of the hospital — we heard the sweet voice of Josephine at last.

It was a promise from God completely and utterly fulfilled, right before my eyes. A tapestry of so many obstacles — my broken past, the abuse to my body, breast cancer, chemotherapy, infertility treatments, having to have a gestational carrier — suddenly gave way to the beauty of the story God had been weaving all along. This child may not have been physically born from my body, but she was knit together by God's stunning grace in our lives and placed into my hands.

The nurses wheeled Josephine and me together into the next room, where we spent the next hour having skin-to-skin contact, followed by another hour of the same with Tim. Our doctor had encouraged us with the plan so that we could avoid scent confusion, making it clear that the first smell of mamma was me.

Now, let it be known, Josephine is pure Savage and made it clear right from the start. Rather than taking breast milk as we hoped, she developed a lactose intolerance and began projectile vomiting any of it we tried to get into her. As she struggled with milk, we struggled with sleep. It turned out that a switch over to formula at the hospital was what she was looking for and we all breathed a sigh of relief.

I tell you, that girl is a Savage. It's going to be on her terms or not at all.

Our long-awaited baby girl was done with waiting. One of the biggest surprises she gave us (besides the projectile milk vomiting) was her attempts to lift up her tiny infant head. Weighing in at eight pounds, two ounces, the hospital staff reminded us that it was far too early for a newborn to be even attempting that.

We told them that she was just a Savage.

But we treasured that little sign up in our hearts. It was like Josephine came out of the womb, alert and aware, knowing that she was going to make an impact on this world. As if she were already conscious of what we had stored up in our hearts for the last 10 years — that the Lord had a purpose and a plan for her.

And the wait was finally over.

Chapter 20

Remembering the Promises

STRENGTH DOESN'T COME FROM what you can *already* do. If that was the truth, doing difficult things would be easy.

Strength actually comes from *overcoming* the things you thought you couldn't do. For me, I am finding strength in the fact that I am more than my past — even more than the redemption of my past — and I'm eagerly looking toward the future, realizing the best is yet to come.

Even still, the rips and tears during the years *after* I gave my life to Christ were real: my battle with cancer, the sorrow of infertility, and the heartbreaking betrayal by friends.

I've learned that giving your life to Christ doesn't eliminate difficulty from your life. However, it does mean that the One who created you is with you through it. In our moments of sorrow, loss, or pain, we can say with the psalmist, "I can never get away from Your presence!" Psalm 139:7 (NLT). His presence and comfort well up from within, providing hope and faith for the future.

For every sad moment we face, God grieves with us.

For every victory and celebration, He celebrates with us.

> The Scriptures describe this as "Christ in you, the hope of glory." (Colossians 1:27 NIV).

I have discovered it to mean that you are *never* alone again in the hard things that come along in life.

The life I tried to knit together for myself needed a serious overhaul — down to the last stitch. As a result, I have been on a constant journey of relearning... almost everything. One of my favorite "discoveries" was what it meant to use my voice for Jesus. I had to do some serious repenting of not speaking up when He gave me revelation. Not stepping further into the call on my life to help others understand and live out the gospel. No more my friend. I will use my voice. Also, singing to the Lord and not just for the sake of singing. Worship has become an ally on those days when it gets really, really hard. That same familiar presence of God is available to me when I sing, and I've discovered He's there as I worship through valleys I never saw coming — like chemo treatments. We can sing because, although this world is broken and hard things happen, we have come to know that God is good and He is always faithful.

Perhaps the thing I can sing loudest about is the stunning fact that I am the daughter of a King.

He rescued me, redeemed me, and saved me from eternal separation from Him.

What That Means For You

Have you, like me, felt like there was a missing piece in your relationship with Jesus?

Or perhaps this is the first time you have heard — really *heard* — about surrendering your life to Jesus. If so, let me clarify what this is really about.

God made everything in the universe. Even you. And He made you to know Him personally, to enjoy an intimate relationship with Him, and to live out a purpose on this earth.

But shortly after God created humanity in the beginning, something went very wrong and sin entered into our lives.

I know "sin" feels like a religious word, but it really just means "miss the mark." It's a term that was historically connected to archery — if your arrow veered to the left or right of the target, you sinned — you missed the mark.

> Romans 3:23 (NIV) says, "For all have sinned and fall short of the glory of God."

When it comes to life, discovering our purpose, and living in a relationship with God, we are all sinners; we have all missed the mark. Sin doesn't necessarily mean you are the worst person you could be, but being a "sinner" does mean there is something inside us that results in chronically missing the mark. For example, God is always on the side of truth. So when we choose to lie — even if it's something small — we conceal the truth; that's sin. Have you ever had anyone ask, "How are you doing?" and your reply was along the lines of "Great! Just dandy." But the reality was you weren't doing great; you were feeling miserable. Perhaps no one was hurt, but you "missed the mark" on speaking the truth – it was a lie just the same, a sin.

If it's true in the small things, it's true in the biggest things as well. When we hate, lust, cheat, break promises, or gossip, we have sinned. We miss the mark on the life we were created for, and we veer further and further away from the God who is "without sin" (1 John 1:5; Hebrews 4:15). How far we have veered away from God's intention for us is really just a matter of degree because we are all in essentially the same position.

Suppose you and I were to each throw a rock and try to hit the moon. You might throw farther than I, but neither of us would come close to hitting it. Our rocks would both fall short in the same way; we all fall short of God's standard.

The growing reality of "missing the mark" and the consequences that come with it leave us with a widening gap in our hearts that we often try to fill with other things. If you've read this far, then you can see clearly for me it was alcohol, drugs, money, acceptance and relationships. For you, it could be shopping, gossiping, using food to control emotions, working until you fall over from exhaustion, or social media. We each find a way to cope, using nearly anything to make ourselves feel whole. But the reality is that there is only One who can fill that emptiness — God Himself, reaching out through the person of Jesus.

The sense of lostness and emptiness would be bad enough if that's all it was, but the news gets worse before it gets better.

> Romans 6:23 (NIV) says, "For the wages of sin is death."

The sinful choices we have made have put us on a trajectory toward death; by sinning, we have "earned" death. It's a frightening thought: there is a death penalty for each person who sins. Not necessarily just physical death either. We're dealing with an eternal God and spiritual realities, so we're looking at a death beyond just the grave. An eternal death.

But now the news gets inconceivably *good*. God knew all this. He saw our predicament and sent His son, Jesus, to live a sinless life — not merely to prove that it could be done — but in a way that counted on our behalf. It's a difficult concept but think of it like this: suppose you were on trial for a crime you had truly committed and someone walked into the courtroom and said, "I may be innocent, but I will go to jail in her place. I will pay the punishment meant for her."

That is what Jesus did. He lived a perfect life here on earth and then was publicly executed like a criminal — crucified on a cross — to pay for all sin. Jesus took the penalty that we deserve for sin, placed it upon Himself, and died in our place.

And why? For *love*.

> Romans 5:8 (NIV) says, "God demonstrates His own love for us in this: While we were still sinners, Christ died for us."

And if that had been all, it would have been amazing but incredibly tragic. Love would have essentially lost — drowned under the weight of so much sin. But three days after His death, Christ came back to life to prove that sin and death had been decisively conquered. God didn't let sin and death have the last word. He raised Jesus to life to put a giant exclamation point on the meaning of His life and death — "the debt has been paid!"

The resurrected Jesus spent the next 40 days on earth, reconnecting with people and revealing what had happened, and then His friends recorded that He "ascended into Heaven" — He returned to the full presence of God — with a promise that His Holy Spirit would soon come to live in his people, guiding them, empowering them, and restoring them to the intention that God originally had for us. The Book of Acts records the fulfillment of all these events.

All of this is a *gift* from God. Totally unearned. There's no "cleaning yourself up" to receive it, no volunteer plan that brings you into a relationship with Him, no "good deed" you can do to earn any of this on your own.

> Ephesians 2:8-9 (NIV) says, "For it is by grace you have been saved, through faith — and this is not from yourselves, it is the gift of God — not by works, so that no one should boast."

"Faith" — another religious word — simply means "trust."

So what do you trust Christ for?

You trust Jesus alone as the source of your forgiveness - the payment and release of your sin — and the One who can give you eternal life. You rely on Him, just like you rely on a chair when you commit your entire weight to a chair to hold you up when you sit down on it. Trusting Jesus is committing the weight of your life, the cost of your sin, your eternal future, and your acceptance with God entirely to Him; there's nothing you're doing to get yourself right with God — Christ does it all.

It's an amazing story, isn't it?

But is it a part of yours?

Perhaps you're thinking:

I'm not too bad. I volunteer at the shelter; I help fight human trafficking; I'm a good person. I even go to church. I don't do anything that's really bad.

Those *are* good things — good living, going to church, helping the poor — but none of it erases sin and restores your relationship with God; it cannot get you to heaven. Eternal life is a gift from God and it only comes through trust in Jesus Christ alone.

Is something keeping you from trusting Christ today? If so, do you know you can ask Him to help you trust? He will help you along the journey, just as He did for me.

But if you know that you are ready — just like I did that day when it felt like God was saying my name — you can respond to God's invitation by simply praying to Him from your heart. The prayer is just a vehicle — no prayer alone saves you — it's just the way you can express your trust in Jesus. He is the one who saves you.

If you would like to put your trust in Jesus to forgive your sin and seal your eternity in heaven, then I'm going to do for you what was done for me — I would like to lead you in that prayer.

Let's be clear, though — it's not about the exact words that you pray. This is about you coming honestly before God with a sincere desire in your heart to be reconciled to Him through Christ and to begin a relationship with Him through faith. This is not something that you have to come back to and re-pray all the time just because you miss the mark in the future and find yourself in sin again. This is a *beginning* — resolving to trust Jesus over yourself, to give your life to Christ with Him in the lead, and to experience His resurrection life for yourself. There are lots of things that you will pray about throughout your future journey with Jesus, but this is about an act of surrender, once and for all, from the heart.

It's a surrender that's ultimately about *receiving.*

Imagine someone selecting an incredible, beautiful, knowing present to give you for Christmas, spending lavish care and time to wrap it and set it under the tree. Yet, on Christmas morning, when you see the present, instead of unwrapping it, you set it on the table in of you and gush over it.

"Oh my gosh, what a beautiful wrapping paper. What beautiful ribbons. You did such a gorgeous job of creating this present for me... I absolutely love it."

Imagine you keep coming back to it day after day to marvel at it, astounded by the gift and the giver, but simply looking at it and never actually choosing to open it.

An unopened present is an unreceived gift.

It doesn't really matter what your religious background is on this point. If you've never set foot in a church or read a Bible, or whether you've been saturated in church your entire life and have a long list of the good things you've done for God — if you haven't received the gift that God freely gave you in Jesus, then it's still a present unopened under the tree.

The gift is there. All you have to do is receive it.

You could begin this relationship with Jesus today. If that is you, maybe your heart is starting to beat a little faster. Maybe you are feeling like you could burst open and cry, or maybe you just know that right now it is your time to surrender your life to Christ.

If that's you, pray this prayer with me:

> *Jesus, I know that I am a sinner, that my life has missed the mark. I admit I have done things that have "missed the mark" for what You intended for my life.*

[In your own words, you can tell Him some of the things that may come to mind]

> *Please forgive me. I trust that You are the Son of God and that You came to die for me on the cross. I receive the free gift of salvation You have given to me. Will You come and live in my heart? Please*

> *lead my life because I know I need You and cannot do it without You. Thank You that, by faith, I can trust You are now taking up residence in my heart. Holy Spirit, invade my heart with Your love, Your guidance, and Your counsel. Thank You, Jesus, for sending Holy Spirit to live in me. Jesus, thank You. Thank You for completing God's plan to give me an eternal relationship with You. I am so grateful that You love me like this. Show me the best ways to follow You throughout all the days of my life. Amen.*

Amen simply means: "Let this be so!"

Did you just honestly pray that to God from your heart? Then I have incredible news for you! The Bible says that your name is now written in the Book of Life. You have just surrendered your life to Jesus and it will prove to be the best decision you have ever made in your life. Your sin — past, present, and future — has been thoroughly forgiven. It no longer separates or distances you from God. Now you get to experience Him for yourself, growing every day as you walk with Him, discovering a life of increasing love, grace, and abundance.

Hear these ancient words from Romans 8:38-39 (NLT) and realize they are true for *you*:

> *And I am convinced that nothing can ever separate us from God's love. Neither death nor life, neither angels nor demons, neither our fears*

> *for today nor our worries about tomorrow—not even the powers of hell can separate us from God's love. No power in the sky above or in the earth below—indeed, nothing in all creation will ever be able to separate us from the love of God that is revealed in Christ Jesus our Lord.*

One of the best things you could do right now is to let someone know.

Let your best friend know. Let your parents know. Let your kids know. Let your pastor know. Let them know that today is the day you gave your life to Jesus and began a whole new life with God.

And, oh my goodness, friend, please let *me* know! You can go to **sandisavage.com/Jesus** and share this incredible news with me. I would love to provide you with some resources to get you started in this relationship with Jesus. There is so much more to come, but today is a day worth celebrating forever! Congratulations, friend. I am so, so excited for you.

Eternity with God does not start when you die. It has already started — today!

Afterword

My friend, if there's any hope I have for this book is that you will realize that it could be the same for you. My prayer has been that, no matter what you have done or what you will do, you will discover the hope, redemption, peace, patience, kindness, and joy that is available to you on the other side of being in a relationship with Jesus.

If you are already in a relationship with Jesus, but your days are long and hard or unforgiving and challenging, then I speak to you as one who has been there myself: remember your first love, your sweet Jesus, that rescued you from eternal death.

He is already with you; remember how to be with Him. Dive into the Word, open up your Bible, and begin reading through the Scriptures. If it's been a while, start with the Gospel of John, then move on to Mark, Ephesians, and wherever you sense yourself being led. I challenge you to read it out loud; let it be one of the loudest voices in your own mouth and ears.

In our journey of walking with Jesus, there are many voices, good and bad, that can direct us on the path our life should take. Even truly good sources — your pastor, a sermon, amazing podcasts, great books — are not a replacement for the voice that speaks to us through the

Bible and through being in a relationship with Jesus. Don't just rely on secondhand revelation from someone else. Dive into the Word and let Him reveal something to you directly. He went through death and resurrection to share this life with you — He is certainly ready and willing to speak to you!

And so that brings us to today. I cannot believe that I get to be the mother to my beautiful toddler baby girl, and married to the hardest-working, loving, caring husband, and father that God could have blessed me with. What does the Lord hold in the future for us? I have no idea, but that's a part of the faith journey. Like any knitter can tell you, at times, things can go all wrong, becoming thoroughly tangled and messy. It seems like nothing good could ever come out right.

But with time, patience, love, grace, and compassion, God will work with you to slowly untangle the threads of your life, knitting together a stunning display of redemption to be lived out in front of others.

My friend, if you're in the midst of a battle, know that the war has already been won by our Lord and Savior, Jesus Christ. Your part is to put your faith in Him and walk out the next right step, day by day.

I write to you as someone who is right there alongside you, fighting the good fight. I hope this story has given you a fresh deposit of hope to keep going. With sincere gratitude and love, thank you for letting me share these pieces of my heart and life with you.

Now, glory be to God in the highest.

He is good all the time, in everything, in every season, and He knit *you* together as a masterpiece.

Acknowledgements

Firstly – I must thank my daughter Josephine. Thank you for inspiring me to be a better mamma and person each and every day. You are pure joy to my heart.

Thank you to my husband Tim. No matter what wild idea I tell you about you are full on supportive for me to chase them. You have shown me each day how to love like Jesus. You are the hardest working, loving husband a woman could ask for. I love and appreciate you so very much.

To my family – I am so thankful to have such a wonderful parents, in laws, brothers and sisters, aunts and uncles, nieces and nephews, cousins and all of our beautiful family. We are certainly blessed.

Justin McCarty – you were sent straight from God to edit this piece of work. After 10 years of ministry together, then 10 years of ministry in different locations it was such a blessing to work with you on this book. Thank you for listening to my endless rambling, sorting through my thoughts and healing parts of my heart I didn't know needed healing. Forever grateful my friend.

To my amazing friends Beth and Jennifer thank you for being my friends. You both hold such a special place in my heart.

To my bestie Greg – What a joy it is to still be friends after over 35 years! You are a constant source of hilarity and grace.

To my pastor Alex Seeley – thank you for helping me see the church with new eyes and always speaking truth in all of our lives.

I wish I could name everyone but it would be an entire other book to list you all.

Above all – thank you Jesus for your death on the cross and resurrection. Thank you Holy Spirit for guiding my way and thank you God for being such a good Father.

Thoughts

Friend, I know when I am trying to work things out in my mind it is helpful to journal, draw pictures or just scribble. Here are a few blank pages for you in case you need to do the same.

About the Author

Sandi Savage is a dynamic author, speaker, cancer survivor and an overcomer of years of abuse and exploitation she experienced while working in the sex industry. She is passionate about equipping people to live a life of freedom through Jesus and telling those stories to the world. With over 20 years of experience in adult ministry she is a voice of wisdom and resilience for those who need to borrow courage to overcome their own life obstacles. Sandi is a ninth-generation Kentuckian, has lived across the globe and currently resides in central Kentucky with her husband Tim, baby girl Josephine, and two diva cats SugarBerri and SnowToe. Learn more about Sandi at sandisavage.com.

Social:

FB: facebook.com/sandrajenelle

IG: instagram.com/sandisavage

Email: sandi@sandisavage.com

Ingram Content Group UK Ltd.
Milton Keynes UK
UKHW012334240723
425713UK00018B/300/J